A Simple Christmas

The Spirit of Simple Living™

A Simple Christmas

A Faith-Filled Guide to a
Meaningful and Stress-Free Christmas

Sharon Hanby-Robie

GuidepostsBooks™
New York, New York

A Simple Christmas

ISBN 0-8249-4703-7

Published by GuidepostsBooks
16 East 34th Street, New York, New York 10016
www.guidepostsbooks.com

Distributed by Ideals Publications, a Guideposts company
535 Metroplex Drive, Suite 250, Nashville, Tennessee 37211

GuidepostsBooks, Ideals, and *The Spirit of Simple Living*
are registered trademarks of Guideposts, Carmel, New York.

ACKNOWLEDGMENTS

Every attempt has been made to credit the sources of copyrighted material used in this book. If any such
acknowledgment has been inadvertently omitted or miscredited, receipt of such information would be appreciated.

All Scripture quotations, unless otherwise noted, are taken from The Holy Bible, New International Version.
Copyright © 1973, 1978, 1984 International Bible Society. Used by permission of Zondervan Bible Publishers.

Scripture quotations marked (KJV) are taken from The King James Version of the Bible.

Scripture quotations marked (NAS) are taken from the New American Standard Bible, © The Lockman
Foundation, 1960, 1962, 1963, 1968, 1971, 1972, 1973, 1975, 1977. Used by permission.

Scripture quotations marked (RSV) are taken from the Revised Standard Version of the Bible. Copyright
© 1946, 1952, 1971 by Division of Christian Education of the National Council of Churches of Christ in the
U.S.A. Used by permission.

Library of Congress Cataloging-in-Publication Data

Hanby-Robie, Sharon.
 A simple Christmas : a faith-filled guide to a meaningful and
stress-free Christmas / Sharon Hanby-Robie.
     p. cm. — (The spirit of simple living)
 Includes bibliographical references (p.   ).
 ISBN 0-8249-4703-7
 1. Christmas. I. Title. II. Series.
 BV45.H36 2006
 263'.915—dc22

                                    2006005589

Cover photograph © gds/zefa/Corbis
Author photograph © Lynn Noble
Designed by Marisa Jackson

Printed and bound in Italy
1 3 5 7 9 10 8 6 4 2

Contents

Introduction

Christmas is the most widely celebrated holiday in the world. The most popular vision of a North American Christmas is an old-fashioned Victorian home nestled in gently falling snow, with children on toboggans or skating on a nearby lake, while a log blazes in the hearth and candles flicker all around. Ivy, holly and mistletoe are strung from every doorway. The turkey is stuffed, the stockings are hung and everyone gathers around the piano with smiles beaming on bright faces as they all sing beloved carols in harmony.

Ah . . . sounds perfect, doesn't it? Or does it? Sadly, today's Christmas sentiment goes more like this: Carolers may be singing and tree lights may be twinkling, but inside my head I am screaming, "Take me away, Calgon!"

Don't despair. There is hope, and some of it is right here in this book. My goal is to help you add a little peace and quiet to your holiday celebrations and make room for meaningful time with loved ones. As you read, you'll find a variety of practical ideas, expert information, and insights from the stories of other people's Christmas experiences. We'll take it one step at a time, beginning with a reminder of what Christmas is all about. Then we'll try to identify the problems that take us off track. For example, if holidays seem too hectic to be enjoyed, perhaps part of the problem is that you have unrealistic expectations about which events should be included. Many of us think a holiday like Christmas should bring us all closer and heal old wounds. Or we may think the holiday will be a marvelous time of charity and goodwill. Then we are disappointed when it falls short.

I will help you appreciate that this extra burden of expectation on top of our already overloaded schedules is not only stressful but also can strain relationships. Have you ever argued with someone over what size tree to buy or at whose home you should celebrate? Under normal circumstances we could settle these disagreements reasonably but because we are all suffering from frazzled nerves, small decisions become very big issues.

As we learn to have reasonable expectations, we can also concentrate on having an enjoyable holiday simply by choosing to live in the stress-free moment and to break the cycle of anxiety. As we come to focus on the good and the wonderful and adopt an attitude of graciousness and thanks, we will learn to make choices that genuinely make sense for the family and the life we have. Whether your family is a blended family, an aging family or a one-person family, you will find useful tips for creating a memorable holiday, including new ideas for warm and glittery holiday décor, easy entertaining, fun activities, better gift giving and more—all without losing your mind or your bank account!

Be encouraged, be of good cheer, and get ready to find the real treasure of the Christmas spirit for one and all.

—*Sharon Hanby-Robie*

A Simple Christmas

PART ONE

O Holy Night: Christmas Attitudes

SOME PEOPLE SPELL CHRISTMAS AS S-T-R-E-S-S, but these holy days are gifts from God through which we stay connected to family and friends. After all, Christmas brings people together who might otherwise drift apart completely. By taking time to evaluate what is important about these special days, we can add purpose to our annual activities and better celebrate the love we have for Jesus and for each other. God never intended that this be a time of anxiety and overwork. Perhaps our expectations are set on the wrong ambitions. So let's take a look at the spiritual meaning of Christmas and the attitudes that can help us keep the holiday simple, and more satisfying too.

The Spiritual Meaning
of Christmas

"The virgin will be with child and will give birth to a son,

and they will call him Immanuel"—

which means, "God with us."

—MATTHEW 1:23

When I think back on the Christmases of my childhood, I barely remember the trees or the presents. They were there, but what I remember most is going to church. I always felt close to God. I cannot remember a time in my life when I did not feel connected to God. As a small child, I knew He was real and that He was with me. Church was always a sanctuary for me. But Christmas at church was special. Christmas was and is holy. It's holy for me, because of the wonder of Christ being born a mere child. God as a child, impossible for some to grasp, yet it was totally believable to me. Maybe that was one of God's purposes for the birth of this holy Child—so that children could relate. I did.

I grew up in the Catholic church, when the Mass was still in Latin. We sang our Christmas carols in Latin too. That was part of the wonder and holiness of Christmas. Simply singing in this ancient language set it apart from the rest of our lives. These hymns and carols express the true meaning of Christmas in a way that purposely engages our spirits in the awesome event of the coming of the Son of God. The poetic conveyance of truths sung reverently lets us join the angels in singing forth His praise. I never really had a singing voice, but that never stopped me from singing full out at church. One year, at the mercy of the choir director, I sang a very short solo (just a refrain) for Christmas midnight services. It was "Silent Night" in Latin. I was thrilled. Just thinking about it brings tears to my eyes now. This was the true meaning of worship to me: to be able to sing with the angels and welcome our Savior to earth.

> The true meaning of worship is being able to sing with the angels and welcome our Savior to earth.

Perhaps that experience is what gave me the courage to take voice lessons when I was forty. I studied for three years and discovered to everyone's amazement that I have a pretty voice. Not great, but pretty. And that is good enough for church singing!

CHRISTMAS IS A TIME TO CELEBRATE CHRIST'S COMING

My heart yearns for the simplicity of the Christmases of my childhood when I could just sit in the church sanctuary and imagine the angels singing as we celebrated Christ's coming. It sounds so easy. Yet somehow, over time, Christmas has turned into a holiday machine that seems nearly impossible to turn off. What was once an intimate and precious experience has turned into a blaze of lights and unrealistic expectations. C. S. Lewis put the dilemma of the modern Christmas in perspective in an essay titled,

"Christmas and Xmas," in which he described the three aspects of Christmas. Christians celebrate the fundamental faith of the holiness of Christmas. But there are two other aspects that have garnered our attention: One involves hospitality and secular merrymaking, and the other is the exercise of charity toward those less well off. These two auxiliary ideas start out with good intentions, but unfortunately, they often morph into an obligation and/or opportunity for impressing people with our entertaining skills and purchasing power.

Amidst the glitter and the glam, the real meaning of Christmas gets diluted. In our effort to enjoy Christmas, we cram our lives with activities. By the time Christmas arrives, we are too exhausted to care. Christmas should be special but not at the expense of the true message of Christmas. Christmas won't make the stingy Scrooge generous, the uncompassionate compassionate, the sad happy, or the angry sweet. Celebrating Christmas is simply a time to remember that the Babe in the manger was born only because he was sent by God the Father to fulfill a mission for us, mere mortals. However we choose to celebrate, our goal should simply be toward a mindfulness of this great miracle.

Luke 2:19 says, "But Mary treasured up all these things and pondered them in her heart." To ponder means to focus your mind and your heart on something specific, in this case, God, His ways, His Word or His will. If we can remember to take the time to ponder these truths, we will experience the true gift of Christmas. If Christmas becomes lost in meaningless jingles and commercial hype, it is because we let it happen. It is only by choice that we can redeem Christmas. Reclaiming Christmas is not about simply placing a crèche in the town square. Christmas must be redeemed first and foremost in our hearts.

To accomplish such a goal, we must be able to identify those things that we value most. If time with family is a valuable part of our Christmas celebration, then

> It is only by choice that we can redeem Christmas.

we must make a conscious choice on how best to accommodate that desire. Christmas cannot be everything, but it can be the best possible if we are selective in our expectations.

Obviously, going to church is one of the most important aspects of Christmas for me. That said, there are times when I have had to choose between church and those I love. This year I desired to attend Christmas services with my niece and sister. But I chose instead to spend quality time on the phone with two dear friends who have battled cancer this year. I disappointed my sister and my niece and missed the worship of singing with the angels, but it was the right choice for me to make. We can make plans to accommodate our greatest desires only when we take time to consider what is most important to us.

SIMPLICITY MADE SIMPLE

TAKE THE TIME TO PONDER and focus on what is important about Christmas for you. What does "Celebrate Christ's Coming" mean to you in terms of what you want Christmas to *be*, rather than what you want to do? Take the time to reflect on the following:

This year I want my Christmas to be . . . (for example, peaceful, happy, hospitable, simple and homespun, simple and elegant)

This Christmas I want my life theme to be . . .

This Christmas I want my heart's theme to be . . .

This Christmas I want my home's theme to be . . .

PRIORITIZE PURPOSES. In *Ladies Home Journal*, Rick Warren identified five key purposes for Christmas: meaningful fellowship, personal growth, helpful service, joyful worship and cheerful sharing. If these were your "Christmas purpose" choices, how would you prioritize them?

As an exercise to focus your mind during Advent, each day think of and **DWELL ON ONE NAME OR ASPECT OF JESUS**: Shepherd, Bread of Life, Water of Life, the Resurrection, the Life, the Way, the Vine . . . . How does this single image remind you of the role of Christ who is with you in this season?

READ LUKE 1–2. Ask yourself: What did God promise? Who did He use to accomplish His plan? What did God say to His people? Why was Jesus born? If you were Mary, what treasures would you have pondered in your heart?

GIVE YOURSELF PERMISSION TO TAKE A BREAK and simply breathe. Set aside ten to fifteen minutes in the next twenty-four hours for this purpose. Find a quiet place without distractions and ask God to help you meditate on Him and refresh your spirit.

ATTEND WORSHIP SERVICES. This is especially needed when you are feeling disconnected. If you don't have a church that you call home, consider returning to the church of your youth or attending services with friends at their church. Remember to make time for joyful worship.

> Lord God, thank You for Your Son, who made
> the way for us. We know that You are always with us,
> but sometimes we simply forget and feel only
> the loneliness. Thank You for setting apart a season
> to remind us of Your holiness, Your glory and
> Your presence in our lives. Lord, help me to focus
> my heart and mind on the gift of Jesus. Amen.

The Promise of Peace

Glory to God in the highest, and on earth peace,
good will toward men.

—LUKE 2:14 (KJV)

The peace on earth that the angels announced to the country shepherds is the same peace the Messiah gives to those on whom God bestows His grace. That peace and goodwill is the promise and true celebration of Christmas.

I can only imagine that it's also what Mary and Joseph wished for in Bethlehem. All those people kept showing up, demanding attention. "We don't want to bother you, but we heard there was a party here." "We hope you don't mind that we didn't call ahead." "We don't want to bother you, but we just stopped by to bring a few gifts." "We thought you might want to know, even the King of Galilee, Herod, might be showing up here." Ever since the first Christmas, the story has been about more than our relationship with God. It has also included a horizontal dimension. People are part of the celebration. Everyone except a real Scrooge knows that people *make* the holiday season into a celebration, but people also complicate the season and add to the stress.

My childhood Christmases were always filled with an abundance of people—mostly family, because I come from such a large one. My grandmother is one of ten children. I could hardly keep track of all the aunts, great aunts and uncles. I do remember Great-Aunt Stella, because my mother often called me Stella. I guess my personality must have reminded her of Aunt Stella. I'm not sure if that was good or bad.

CHRISTMAS IS A TIME TO CELEBRATE WITH PEOPLE WE LOVE

Let's assume we have a bit more control over our lives than did Mary and Joseph, though some may question this assumption. First we must decide *with whom* we want to have Christmas-season fellowship. Worthwhile fellowship requires heart-to-heart sharing, and honest communication is necessary for family and friends to grow closer to each other. That kind of sharing cannot be orchestrated with everyone you know. It demands being selective with your time and purposefully selecting those with whom you will spend time on Christmas Day, as well as throughout the busy weeks of December.

With most families there are riffs and tiffs that surface, particularly during the holidays. Part of the problem is our expectation that holidays should make for peace and harmony. But in reality, if you never got along with Uncle George, why do you think you would on Christmas Day? It's unrealistic. So prepare yourself not to be upset. Plan in advance to act like a duck and let his comments roll off your back like water. Sometimes the easiest way to avoid confrontation is to keep some members of the family separate from each other.

This year I purposely chose to make Christmas simple. To spend quality time with those I love, I scheduled intimate Christmas celebrations with the individuals most important to me. By giving each family or friend a special evening, I was able to focus my attention on each one alone, thus avoiding jealousies. I was able to prepare friends' favorite meals and celebrate with each personally. My goddaughter asked for chicken corn chowder and a quiet evening with just my husband and me. It was wonderful. My in-laws preferred celebrating at their home rather than mine. I brought part of the meal, and they prepared the rest.

We'll revisit the topic of "who" in later discussions of party guest lists and gift giving, but for now, right at the beginning of a book about celebrating a simple Christmas, let's take a good look at some basic "who" issues.

Set obligations aside for a minute and then ask yourself: Who energizes me? Who makes me feel at peace? Who helps me remember "the reason for the season"? Krissy and I have been friends since we were three years old. Krissy is one of the funniest and most resilient people I know. I believe that she knows me as well as she knows herself. Spending time with her is always a pleasure I treasure. She makes me laugh, cry and simply appreciate life. When I return home to Ohio for the holidays, it's always a rush and a blur, but that will never stop me from finding time to visit with this dear friend.

Of course we have real obligations to some people, especially those in our immediate family. And I choose to reach out to others, even though I am not obligated to do so. After all, Christmas is celebrating God's great generosity to us and God asks us to be generous with others. Sorting out "people priorities" is part of my holiday planning, every year. Sometimes last year's obligations or generosities do not need to be this year's priorities. Last year you might have found time for Christmas tea with your child's playmate's mother, but is it necessary this year?

May I also suggest that you give priority to making time to reconcile with at least one person—to spread "peace on earth"? Unless we learn to forgive, we will spend every Christmas celebrating with an underlying tension that prevents us from

> Be selective in determining with whom you will spend time on Christmas Day.

enjoying the gift of the season. When it comes to peace, the best place to practice it is within our own families. Why? Because one of the most stressful realities of holiday celebration centers around the unresolved hurts, unsettled conflicts, painful memories and uncomfortable relationships that often exist within the family.

Christmas is a time for reconciliation. Jesus came to restore our broken relationships with God and with others. Only when we have made peace with others can we truly give thanks and celebrate in joyful worship of Jesus—the true Christmas gift—the Christ.

Terry Helwig discovered the peace of fellowship in a Christmas Eve ritual at her church. Maybe her story will inspire you to share the peace—and light—of Christ in this winter season.

Today is Christmas Eve. The grandfather clock in the hall dongs six times. And in the still shadows of early morning, I light the fifth candle on my Advent wreath.

The fifth candle, the Christ candle, plays an important role in our church's Christmas Eve service. Late in the service, our minister takes a small, unlit candle and approaches the altar where the Christ candle burns. Lighting his candle in its flame, he begins the passing of that flame.

I remember last year how candlelight reflected off his glasses as he carried his flame toward the two ushers waiting to pass the flame to the congregation. Rustling noises filled the pews as everyone readied their candles. My husband Jim lifted his candle toward the usher, then turned and passed his flame to our daughter Mandy, sitting beside him. Mandy tilted her candle toward me. A drop of warm wax fell on my hand as my candle burst into flame. Then I turned and edged toward the man sitting beside me. In every pew, neighbor turned to neighbor. And gradually, one by one, the entire sanctuary filled with the flickering light of two hundred tiny flames. Looking again at the Christ candle, burning serenely at the front of the church, I realized that each of us had symbolically received and passed on the love of Christ.

The powerful symbolism of that moment remains with me, even now, as I journey toward my inner Bethlehem. Staring into the flames of my Advent wreath, this Christmas Eve, I discover the sleeping candle of Christ deep within me. And as I light the Christ candle within, I know a thousand other flames can spring from it, if only I am willing to share that light.

And perhaps sharing that light is easier than I think. I remember caroling last week at the convalescent home where a frail gentleman was seated in a wheelchair in front of me. He wore a bulky gray sweater that made him look like a giraffe in elephant's clothing. His mouth gaped in a smile until a nurse unknowingly knocked off one of his navy blue slippers. She was gone before he could protest. As we sang, his black-stocking foot fished unsuccessfully on the floor for his slipper. Minutes passed. His foot kept moving. Then blushing, I stepped forward, knelt beside him and pulled the slipper onto his foot. I thought of Jesus washing the disciples' feet saying, "[I] came not to be served but to serve" (Matthew 20:28, RSV). When I looked up, the man's grateful eyes met mine and something passed between us. I think it was the flame of the Christ candle.

It seems that the flame can be passed quite simply . . . by washing a foot or slipping on a shoe. Perhaps, as Mother Teresa said, "It is not how much we do, but how much love we put into the doing."

SIMPLICITY MADE SIMPLE

SIMPLY FORGIVE. Forgiveness is the most valuable gift we can give anyone, including ourselves. Forgiving is a lesson in growth. By forgiving we create an opportunity to grow into the kind of person God designed us to be.

BE KIND. Look for opportunities to do simple acts of kindness. The stress of the holidays leaves a lot of people operating on their last nerve. A little unexpected kindness can make a difference.

Actress Jamie Lee Curtis says, "The holidays are a time to create memories that have nothing to do with things bought, but only with the things taught and shared." She enjoys "clinging to the holidays **AS A TIME OF CONNECTION** to my family, friends and loved ones."

As discussed in this chapter, **ASK YOURSELF WHO ENERGIZES YOU** and try to spend time with that person, maybe in a way that helps you both accomplish some holiday task—shopping together, baking together or even worshiping together.

EVALUATE YOUR FELLOWSHIP PRIORITIES in light of your Christmas purposes. Is Christmas a time to celebrate the birth of Christ? Is it a time to be a peacemaker within your own family? Is it a time to enjoy being with your immediate family? Is it a time to create a beautiful and inviting home environment to share with others? Is it a time to exchange gifts and be generous? Is it a time to help those less fortunate? Is it is a time to strengthen bonds with family and friends? Or a time to take a break and relax? What do your answers say about your people priorities?

LIGHT AN ADVENT PEACE CANDLE. One explanation of the colored candles on an Advent wreath says that they represent Hope, Peace, Joy and Love—the Peace candle being lit on the third Sunday before Christmas. Think of that Sunday as being a peacemaking day, setting the tone for the holiday itself.

> Lord, I know that I must be at peace with others
> in order to have real communion with You.
> Help me to use the seasons of celebration
> as holy days of reconciliation with people
> You have placed in my life. May Your love always
> shine through mine. Amen.

The Myth of the Perfect Christmas

> To sum up, let all be harmonious, sympathetic, brotherly, kindhearted, and humble in spirit.
>
> —1 PETER 3:8 (NAS)

I hate fake Christmas trees, but I am seriously considering buying one anyway. I am simply tired of the annual argument that my husband and I have as we attempt to position the real tree so that it stands one hundred percent straight! Part of the problem is that this is not something I can physically do myself. The other part of the problem is that it is something that my husband just doesn't have much patience for. The bigger problem is that, despite this, he insists that we put up a tree.

Quite frankly, as much as I love the smell, look and atmosphere that a Christmas tree brings to our home, I am usually too stressed and too busy to even want to fuss with it. You see, the only part of the Christmas tree that my husband deals with is the part we fight about—getting it into the stand. The decorating, undecorating and repacking of all the ornaments is left up to me. In addition, we spend so little time during the holidays at home that I hardly get to enjoy it. If I had a fake little tree that simply popped up—lights and all—it would surely take some of the stress out of this part of the holiday. But I hate fake Christmas trees. . . .

Among the top complaints about the holidays are the increased expectations on our time and our obligations to buy gifts, go to parties and travel. These extra burdens along with our already overloaded schedules are stressful because everyone is suffering from frazzled nerves, but they can also create relationship issues (like our yearly struggle over a lopsided tree). Sadly, most of us don't realize that the root problem is that our expectations for a perfect Christmas are entirely too grand.

Neither do we realize that we have set ourselves up to be disappointed. Yes, the media and the retailers certainly play along with our silly game of unrealistic expectations, but we have choreographed our own failure from the time we planned the first Christmas together—with our mate or our child or our grandchild. We wanted that memory to be filled with tantalizing aromas, delicious foods and beautiful decorations. And once we turned that first holiday into something unforgettable, we didn't want to disappoint our loved ones the next year. So now we continue to attempt to outdo ourselves each year. And when our sweet but now elderly parents are no longer able to contribute their part to the Christmas extravaganza, we add their seasoned list of duties to our own.

In our hearts, we are yearning for a simpler yet significant way to celebrate this special day, but we don't have any idea how to stop our Christmas machine. The result is, as Garrison Keillor, author and public radio personality, says, "The lovely thing about Christmas is that it's compulsory, like a thunderstorm, and we all go through it together."

PERFECTION ISN'T NEEDED FOR A
PERFECTLY WONDERFUL HOLIDAY

In his book *A Recipe for Christmas*, Handel H. Brown says that "the secret of Christmas joy is love and friendliness—a love and a friendliness which are not so obvious at other times of the year." That may be true for some, but I suspect that the pressure to be loving and friendly simply adds to the stress for many people. The reality is that unless we develop realistic expectations about the holidays, we will continue to be stressed and disappointed with the results.

> Unless we develop realistic expectations about the holidays, we will continue to be disappointed with the results.

The myth of the perfect Christmas also touches the reality of the people who "make" Christmas for us— our family and even those friends, acquaintances or strangers who drop by unexpectedly bringing us gold, frankincense or myrrh. (Wouldn't we wish?) The truth is that our networks—colleagues, friends, families—are composed of imperfect people. And it's good for every one of us to admit that we ourselves are among the flawed—among the people Jesus came to earth to save. If you need perfection, maybe you should invest in a company that can design and manufacture the perfect robot. Hmm, I wonder if there's a catalog from which I can order a perfect husband! Probably not.

For me, I either have to learn to be happy with a fake Christmas tree or simply accept the fact that as long as the real tree doesn't fall down, a little leaning is just fine. PS: I finally gave in this year, and bought a fake tree. And, much to my surprise, it turned out to be one of the most beautiful trees I have ever had!

The key is convincing yourself and then communicating with loved ones that just as there are no perfect people, there are no perfect holidays—and that is perfectly okay.

Pam Kidd faced this reality one year as her family was decorating. She explains:

By the second Sunday in Advent, decorating Kidd-style is in full swing. "Keep moving or Mom will decorate you," my husband David teases the kids, but I'm too consumed with seeking perfection to laugh.

"Put the heaviest ornaments on the bottom of the tree, Keri. Brock, can't you remember how we always arrange the greenery on the mantel? David, would you get the rest of the stuff from the attic? No, I don't have time to cook supper. Why don't you order a pizza?"

Dashing through the dining room with my arms full of garland, I pause to find Keri sitting there. "Mama," she asks, "do you remember this old Snoopy ornament?"

Remember? How could I forget?

Of course there was a story behind the fifteen-year-old ornament. An amusement park. A Santa Claus. A Snoopy toy. And suddenly, a memory slows Pam down. She gives a second look to her college-aged daughter, who is "probably a bit weary of being ordered around by a mom who has lost her focus." Soon the whole family is eating pizza and reminiscing.

Pam concludes, reflecting on the choice before her: "I can run myself ragged trying to create a picture-perfect Christmas, or I can relax and bask in the glow of good times pulled from our memories of Christmas past, memories that light the way to the real Christmas."

SIMPLICITY MADE SIMPLE

ADJUST YOUR PERCEPTION OF PERFECTION. Most of our ideas for the "perfect" Christmas come from what we think existed in holidays gone by. For example, we think that the old-fashioned Christmas is what we should be recreating. The reality is that the old-fashioned Christmas was just for children. Adults did not exchange gifts, and there wasn't the hullabaloo around making everything picture-perfect that media emulate today. In an old-fashioned Christmas, people simply enjoyed one another. The other problematic perception is the one we carry around in our heads from childhood. It's easy to remember a wonderful Christmas experience from our youth, because we didn't have to clean, shop, cook and wrap all those presents—we just enjoyed ourselves! Recognizing that our perception might need a new pair of eyeglasses is winning half the battle to reach our goal: enjoying a simply wonderful holiday.

Sometimes we compound the problem by not communicating our expectations to others. Just because we have always done something one way doesn't mean it is the only—or even the best—way to spend the holiday. **TAKE THE TIME TO TALK THINGS OVER.** Sometimes this simple act can keep everyone from being disappointed. Too often, we are afraid to talk about things, because we think we know how people are going to react. Instead, we must give people the benefit of the doubt and explain the reasons why we want to do things differently than we have in the past. Often, when others see that we are sincere and are truly trying to make things better for everyone, they understand and support changes in tradition.

Recognize that **IT'S OKAY TO FEEL THE WAY YOU DO.** It's okay if just thinking about the holidays puts your head into a spin. Give yourself permission to feel whatever you feel; you don't have to justify emotions—they simply exist. You can, however, change your expectations, and that will often go a long way toward changing how you feel too. Don't judge yourself or compare your holiday attitude to others' feelings or actions. We are different from one another, and we react differently to circumstances. What one person finds energizing, another can find exhausting—but even that is okay!

DON'T LOSE YOUR SENSE OF HUMOR. In times of chaos and stress, humor can be your most important resource. Learn to laugh at yourself. Very little will ruin your day when you can laugh about it. Laughing at a crooked tree just might help me with my "issue"!

LET GO OF PERFECTION. Only God can achieve perfection, so stop trying to compete with Him, because you won't win. It doesn't matter if there is a spot on the tablecloth; that is not what is important. The spirit of celebration and the fellowship are what matter most. My mother taught me a valuable lesson: If the house is filled with people, food and laughter, no one will notice the handprints on the wall.

NAME AND EXPLAIN ONE EXPECTATION of perfection that you want to let go of this year in order to simplify your celebration.

> Lord, You are the One who called us
> to celebrate Your love. Filter my vision to see
> food, fun and festivities as simply a grand way
> to fellowship with family, regardless of how far
> from perfection our efforts seem. Amen.

Reining in Christmas Competition

My crown is in my heart, not on my head;
Not decked with diamonds and Indian stones,
Not to be seen: my crown is called content.

—WILLIAM SHAKESPEARE, *HENRY VI*

I love my job at QVC as the resident home décor expert, but I will admit that Christmas is a very long season there, just as it is at most retail stores. We announce Christmas in July, and by September we are counting down the days until its arrival. Fourth quarter is our busiest season, which means no vacation during this time. As a result, by the time Christmas actually arrives, most of us are a bit bleary-eyed. Just thinking of all the holiday commotion makes me want to turn into a Scrooge. The decorating, card sending, gift exchanging, entertaining and happy carols playing incessantly on the radio can make me feel like crawling under the covers and avoiding the rest of the season. Part of the reason I dread the season is because it has become such a fierce competition.

Why do we insist on trying to outdo ourselves every year? I realize that part of the pressure comes from our desire to make others feel happy and appreciated. But a lot of it also comes from all the retailers and their mega-advertising campaigns. You can't walk into a mall, grocery store or even pet shop without being subjected to jingles with agendas to get you to buy more, do more and eat more. Ugh! Do my cats really need cookies with little red ribbons? No. But I continue to fall prey to the retailing magic. This year I presented Miss Peony and Sir Percival with a little hedgehog pull-toy. They looked at it and at me as if we were out of our minds, which obviously I must have been when I bought it.

It's no wonder, considering my work at QVC, that when it comes to decorating for Christmas, especially outdoors, I stick with the very basics. I instruct my sweet hubby to hang the icicle lights on the back porch, and install one spotlight pointed at the front door where I hang a wreath—simple and more than enough for me.

But I must say that this year I found the super-large inflatable snow globes with their falling snow inside nearly irresistible. I had never thought outdoor Christmas lawn ornaments to be cute, but these . . . .

Some people take their decorating so seriously that it can become an intense competition in itself. A December 18, 2005 article in the *Washington Post* noted the decoration sparring evident at the Maryland and Virginia governors' mansions. The paper ran a chart comparing the decorations as if it were a football game. For example, "Feet of garland, artificial: Maryland 200, Virginia 0"; "Feet of garland, natural: Maryland 0, Virginia 150." Natural garland aside, the Maryland mansion far outstripped the Virginia mansion, but then the Maryland governor was up for reelection and the Virginia governor wasn't!

My attitude—unless you're running for governor, don't get caught up in the neighborhood outdoor-lighting competition. On the other hand, if you find decorating exhilarating, go ahead, climb that ladder, hang those lights, wrap every single branch and eave to your heart's content. But if you find decorating a chore at best, you have my permission to turn off your house lights at 5:00 PM and pretend you have left town for the season!

Christmas is a time of good cheer, and the decorations, Christmas cards and gift giving are all part of the holiday spirit. But it's easy to cross the line from good-will to excess. The who, what, where, how much and why of holiday hurry is up to you. Start by figuring out how much time, effort and money you are willing to allot to such things.

It might surprise you to learn that the first Christmas tree with electric lights belonged to Edward H. Johnson, an associate of inventor Thomas Edison. He proudly displayed his Christmas tree, hand-wired with eighty red, white and blue electric light bulbs the size of walnuts, on December 22, 1882, at his home on Fifth Avenue in New York City. The local newspapers ignored it, seeing it as a publicity stunt to sell those little light bulbs. But a Detroit newspaper reporter published it, and . . . the rest is history. I tell you this so you don't feel compelled to continue what started out as a way of selling more goods.

> ## Why do we insist on trying to outdo ourselves every year?

Following my own motto to live simply, I struggle every year with the idea of sending Christmas cards. Selecting and sending Christmas cards is a task I find filled with guilt, confusion and irritation. I am frustrated by friends who have the time to take their lists and cards to the beach for a weekend of addressing. (Okay, I admit that I am a bit envious that they are getting off to the beach while I drive to work fighting blinding snow.) I become stress filled and guilt ridden as I read the three-page newsletters from people who have more free time than I can imagine. And yet I do love hearing from friends far away whom I otherwise rarely see or get mail from. It's a great way to reconnect as we wait for a time when we can again spend time together.

I also know how much young children love receiving mail addressed to them. So my Christmas card list, though quite small, always includes the youngest loved ones. I keep my list manageable, despite the fact that I feel a pang of guilt when I open cards from people not on my list.

GUESTS AND GIFTS

Holiday entertaining is supposed to offer us an opportunity to spend quality time with those we love. But it too can become an oppressive competition. My attitude about entertaining is the same as for decorating. If you aren't a "formal fancy," don't pretend to be one. Neither you nor your guests will enjoy it. When I work with clients, I design their homes to meet their lifestyles. The same goes for entertaining. I give you permission to make a big pot of chili and let people serve themselves. At my house the kitchen is the heart of the home. Guests invariably end up in the kitchen with me as I cook. I put the willing and able to work with me, and let the others work on enjoying the hors d'oeuvres.

When it comes to gift giving, many of us are feeling the pressures of over-consumerism. The commercialization of Christmas and the focus on accumulating and giving material things is making us feel exploited. There is no shortage of Bible passages that call on us to show restraint and not hoard goods. Most of us have enough, and to simply keep adding to our piles feels wrong. If we are to follow Christ's example, we would live simply and aspire for an attitude of "enough."

A new movement has dedicated itself to saying "enough" and to reviving the original meaning of Christmas giving. Buy Nothing Christmas is a nationwide initiative started by Canadian Mennonites but open to everyone with a thirst for change and a desire for action. It started in 2001 and has since grown exponentially with a Web site (www.buynothingchristmas.org) and a network of organizers. They admit that most of us will have to buy "something." But when you do buy, they encourage you to remember principles such as buying locally, buying "fair trade," noting environmentally friendly packaging, recycling or reusing and buying items that last. The main aim is to slow down the pace of Christmas and to challenge our overly consumptive lifestyle.

My friend Jan has always considered "gifting" to be one of her gifts. She takes great pride in choosing gifts. This past year was financially challenging for her, and in early December she suggested we skip buying gifts for each other. I told her it was too late for me to skip (I had already purchased hers), but she could and should not buy a gift for me. But her heart could not resist. Only Jan could find the perfect gift while sitting at the hospital, waiting to hear results of her grandbaby's heart surgery. As she waited her eyes caught the sparkle of four glass-beaded ornaments shining in the sunlight. They are perfect for me. I love them. But next year I'll be sure that she and I decide well in advance whether we will "gift" or "not gift." As far as I am concerned, her friendship is more than gift enough.

SIMPLICITY MADE SIMPLE

BE SELECTIVE IN YOUR HOLIDAY DÉCOR. Decorating for the holidays is supposed to get you in the mood for a happy and memorable celebration. If you instead find yourself in a Scrooge mood as you struggle to hang the tangled mass of lights, take the time to evaluate how necessary it really is to your celebration. Ask yourself why you are doing this. Are you self-motivated, or are you doing it to keep up with the neighbors? Is it to carry on a tradition? If so, does your family really care about this tradition? A typical family spends $215 a year on new decorations.

Think about how you could better bless your family with this money, if decorations aren't a priority for you.

"DO" CHRISTMAS ONLY TO THE AMOUNT OF ENERGY YOU HAVE this year. You don't have to run yourself ragged every year. People who love you don't expect you to. Keep things in perspective. Just because you have "always" done such and such doesn't mean you have to do it now. In the years when you can put more effort in it, do it because you want to. Some years you can give more; in other years, give yourself a break.

Remember that **THE BEST GIFTS DON'T COME IN PACKAGES**. Consider some of these alternatives: Make a reduced copy of your marriage license for your spouse's wallet; write a poem for your loved one; fix a really great breakfast for your spouse and serve it in bed; rent a romantic movie and watch it with your partner; work on a puzzle together; make a batch of your grandchild's favorite cookies; put a note in a balloon for each child on your list, saying what you appreciate most about him or her.

REDUCE THE COST OF SENDING CHRISTMAS CARDS. The best way is by not sending them in the first place. To what names on your list can you e-mail a holiday greeting? Consider a surprise phone call instead of a card. Send postcards instead of cards; they are cheaper to mail and just as effective. Make card sending a family activity. Let older children help with addressing, signing and stamping the envelopes. Younger children can decorate the envelopes with stickers. If you are really pressed for time but still want to send cards, let Hallmark do the work for you. Log on to www.Hallmark.com. You can order your cards online and even have Hallmark print your name and holiday message, address the cards and mail them for you. If you'd rather handwrite a note, Hallmark will print your names and address the cards, then ship them to your home for your personal touch. One more tip: Don't worry about making the Christmas deadline. Most friends would be thrilled to hear from you, even if it's not until New Year's Eve!

God, help me to remember that we are called
to live in opposition to the norms and assumptions
of this culture of consumption. Give me wisdom
in determining what I truly need and help me
to decide what is not essential to celebrate
joyfully this Christmas. Amen.

The Secret of Personal De-stress

Look, there on the mountains, the feet of one who brings
good news, who proclaims peace! Celebrate your festivals,
O Judah, and fulfill your vows. . . .

—NAHUM 1:15

Nahum's proclamation of peace in the above quote is complete with encouragement to celebrate our festivals. The picture that this good news creates is one of joy and complete restoration of the Lord's great plan for His people. Although this verse is not specifically about Christmas, it is a good example of how God wants us to celebrate holy festivals. Feasts or festivals were religious observances that conveyed joyful celebration—and what could be more joyous than celebrating the birth of our Lord? That is, unless we are too tired and too stressed to even smile!

Where are those "Kodak moments" that people talk about? Even if we have established in our minds the fact that there is no such thing as a perfect holiday, the

Christmas season can still be stressful. In fact, a Gallup poll of 1,001 Americans revealed that almost half of those surveyed, forty-eight percent, reported experiencing some degree of stress during the holidays, and fifty-five percent also reported losing sleep. It isn't surprising that more women than men experienced holiday-time insomnia (fifty-two percent versus thirty-eight percent respectively). And women were almost twice as likely as men to report feeling "exhausted" after the holiday hustle and bustle! Perhaps it's because men don't feel compelled to make everyone happy and meet every little expectation. It's quite easy for them to find a comfortable chair and watch the football game rather than fretting about the perfect bow on Aunt Edna's gift.

Part of the problem is also that stress has become such a given in modern life that many of us assume that tension and anxieties are unavoidable. Although our stress thresholds are as unique as each individual, there is a point when we do become overstressed and exceed our coping capabilities. The sheer number of demands made on us during the holiday season is more than most of us can handle without feeling overwhelmed. As our stress response is engaged over and over again with no time for rest, our warm feelings of goodwill toward man quickly turn to competition over the last parking space in the lot!

CONTROLLING THE STRESS

Let's admit that we wouldn't really want a totally stress-free life. A stress-free existence would be analogous to a lifelong drive on black ice. Friction is what allows us to control the cars we drive and walk our town sidewalks. A little interplay and stress as we go about our lives keeps us from boredom and actually can energize our days. As they claim with cholesterol, there's the good variety and the bad.

I'm talking here about "bad" stress, which overwhelms us emotionally, spiritually and even physically. And much of it has to do with control issues. We want what we want when we want it. Dr. Morton C. Orman, who specializes in teaching how to eliminate stress, says, "When people don't behave as we want during the holidays . . . we often set out to change or control their behavior." When that doesn't work, we get frustrated. So "it's not just the behavior of others . . . that drives us crazy . . . but rather that people fail to think, feel or behave exactly as we want."

Most of us don't realize that we are the source of our own "bad" holiday stress. We may not be able to control others, but we have the ability to control our own stress; stress is an option we choose in processing unpleasant events. For example, how you choose to react is up to you when you are stuck in line behind someone who can't find her checkbook and also needs to have each gift packaged separately while going through the receipt to verify that she was given all the applicable discounts. You can either blame the person in front of you for the stress you feel (and make matters worse), or you can remind yourself that you are choosing to live a stress-free moment and break the cycle of anxiety.

> Most of us don't realize that we are the source of our own "bad" holiday stress.

Millions of Americans live by what is known as the "serenity prayer": "Lord, grant me the serenity to accept the things I cannot change; courage to change the things I can; and wisdom to know the difference." And the attitude expressed in that prayer, by Reinhold Niebuhr, is the secret to de-stressing the Christmas season. What can we change? Ourselves, with God's help.

What can I do when I'm standing behind that woman in the store line? I can take a deep breath and push the negative attitude and thoughts from my mind. I can choose to concentrate on how enjoyable the holiday is going to be with my family and be grateful that I am not as problematic or compulsive as she is. Besides, I can consider this a time of blessing and an opportunity to improve my brain by balancing my checkbook without a calculator. (Time will pass real quickly doing this!) Or I can choose to share the spirit of the season with the person behind me; who knows, I may find a new friend.

Stress can also be relieved by getting enough sleep. Getting as little as an hour less sleep than we need affects how we function in the course of a day, creating situations that contribute significantly to our stress. A. Christopher Hammon, director of the Center for Sleep and Stress, says, "Getting the sleep we need plays a key role in the amount of stress we can handle through the day before becoming over-stressed. It is during sleep that our brain sorts through information taken in through the day, and works toward resolving emotional issues that have come up."

In a later chapter we'll deal with holiday depression. I'm not suggesting you sleep away the month of December, but sleep is a bit like prayer and Bible reading, without it the Christmas season can start to fall apart.

Early in December Carol Kuykendall usually sensed the drag of holiday fatigue. But one year an Advent talk at her church turned her holidays around and gave her new energy. She explains:

> "Every year we vow things will be different," the speaker said, "and every year we find ourselves facing the same responsibilities. The truth is we can't change many of our Christmas obligations, but we can change our attitudes by remembering why we're doing all these things. Christmas gives us opportunities to show our love."
>
> Just before she sat down the speaker quoted a line from Victor Hugo's *Les Misérables* that became the theme of my Christmas preparation: "To love another is to see the face of God."
>
> A few days later, when my sister called unexpectedly from California to say she and her family could join us over Christmas, I didn't think about the extra obligations that lay ahead. I thought about the great

opportunity for a four-day family reunion: the opportunity to come up with unique gift ideas, which led to the opportunity to sort through a huge box of old photos and make an album for each family, telling the chronological story of our childhood Christmases.

From that point forward, while my days were full, they were not draining. And as these acts of love became opportunities, I felt energized.

Responsibility or opportunity? Sometimes your attitude is all that makes the difference.

SIMPLICITY MADE SIMPLE

GET ENOUGH SLEEP. To do so, avoid overeating at night. Keep a pad of paper and a pencil by your bed. If you're afraid you're not going to remember something that just came to mind—something you just must do tomorrow, someone you must call—write down an assignment to yourself. Then put it out of your mind. Or try singing carols to yourself. Or praying—maybe the serenity prayer. Carry on an imaginary conversation with Mary or Joseph or Baby Jesus. If an at-home task feels overwhelming, get up and work on it for only fifteen minutes, then come back to bed, feeling some assurance that you made a bit of progress.

MAKE TIME FOR EXERCISE. Most people tend to reduce or even stop their workout regimens during the holidays despite the fact that we know that exercise is one of the best available stress reducers and sleep enhancers.

CAST THE BURDEN. Claim the promise. Try memorizing this short Scripture verse and repeating it as often as necessary. The "him," of course, refers to God: "Cast all your anxiety on him because he cares for you" (1 Peter 5:7).

GET ORGANIZED. To do so, start with some basic tools—a journal, day-timer, calendar or palm computer in which you can keep schedules and make notes. Nothing increases stress as much as losing the envelope on which you wrote that important phone number. In terms of organizing, even on a daily basis, identify the things you want to do and the things you need to do. Then prioritize the list. Once organized, you can manage and budget your time to accommodate what really matters.

At all times, keep in your purse or tote bag something that can help you **"REDEEM" TIME THAT MIGHT OTHERWISE BE "WASTED"**—standing in lines, waiting in a doctor's office and so forth. That something might be anything from a book to unopened mail.

MAKE A LIST OF STRESS TRIGGERS you can try to avoid. Does one store always have long lines? Go to another. Even if you can't go to a different store, being aware of potential irritations reduces the power they hold over us. Rather than simply responding with stress, we can prepare ourselves to avoid a quick, negative response. "The more we understand our reactions to the people and situations that cause us stress, the more creative and productive our reactions become," Hammon notes.

> Lord, help me distinguish between what I can
> control and what is beyond my reach. Help me
> to lay aside anxiety over what is left undone
> in order to truly rest in the joy of Your love. Amen.

The Big Family Gathering:
Attendance Required?

The Lord then said to Noah, "Go into the ark,

you and your whole family. . . ."

—GENESIS 7:1

When it comes to spending time with our families during the holidays, it can sometimes feel like we are expected to set off together on the ark. How would you and your family fare if God commanded you to confine yourselves to a boat for a few months? And don't forget all the animals that were also on this little cruise. The noise, the smell, the chaos—all adding to the family festival of stress! That's how it is for some extended families. Instead of enjoying one another, they have more disagreements and feel overwhelmed. Perhaps it is because there are so many decisions to make and extra activities to schedule. Add to that the worries of finances, and holidays can bring out the worst in even the best families.

Just because we love each other doesn't mean that spending Christmas together is the best thing to do. There is no commandment that says you must spend your holiday by ducking potshots from your Uncle George about the way you dress or how you spend your money. It makes far more sense to consider family problems when planning gatherings.

For example, if you know that certain family members do not get along well, take the time to resolve the situation before you get together. Christmas dinner is not the time to make up. And leaving things to chance often causes more problems and makes things worse. The mere fact that you are already dreading the family holiday gathering is a tell-tale sign that things are not going to go well. Stop and think about it: Much of the stress surrounding the holidays is preventable.

Coming from a large family, I know something about sibling issues. A few years ago, one of my sisters apparently had a problem with me. Rather than talking it out, she seemed to vent an unknown anger toward me the few times a year that we saw each other. I felt as if I was being verbally attacked. Eventually I tried to stay away from her. Last year, when I couldn't avoid seeing her, I simply tried to give her my best attitude. Things went better, not perfectly, but a kind spirit definitely lightened the air.

This year, the morning after I arrived at my mother's for a holiday celebration, my sister phoned, wanting to know why I hadn't told her I was in town. We talked a few things over, and, though I don't think I will ever know what prompted her original attacks, we made a pact to try harder with each other. And this year, I will say that there was no squabbling between us. We're looking to the future and thanking God for grace.

> Just because we love each other doesn't mean that spending Christmas together is the best thing to do.

PREPARE FOR THE BEST EXPERIENCE

Relationship expert Keith Varnum says that there are simple strategies that will not only help you survive the traditional family Christmas visit but also enable you to actually enjoy it. He commends the Boy Scouts motto, "Be Prepared!" and encourages forming alliances with brothers and sisters and other relatives who are sympathetic to your plight. It can be as simple as agreeing to run interference for each other. Varnum even suggests that you "hold mock question-and-answer sessions with your allies to practice gracefully fending off the slings and arrows. Prepare for cross-examination." That way you will have your answers ready for the questions you know you are sensitive to or touchy about.

The best defense is always a good offense. Prepare a list of questions to be used as responses to throw Uncle George off the subject. If you and your younger sister are still fighting over childhood rivalries, adopt a bit of humor and dance around the old land mine instead of walking into it. It's also a good idea to have an exit strategy ready just in case conversations get too heated. Warn your family in advance that you might have to cut your visit short. It is far better to be honest about how much time you can spend with your family and still enjoy them than it is to end up bored and bothered, or burdened with resentful feelings.

Set a realistic expectation. Sometimes the reality is that the best we can hope for is "surviving" the holiday gathering rather than getting everyone to be happy about it. If family dynamics are especially difficult, Keith Varnum recommends an attitude summarized as "Be of good cheer, the end is near! . . . You don't have to stay any longer than you can keep on top of the ruckus. Be lighthearted, playful and flexible—and enjoy the family circus as much as you can!"

Watch for danger signs, especially between you and your immediate family. If you and your spouse find that you are retreating from each other or are being irritable about everything, schedule some quiet time together to talk about it. Even fifteen minutes can make a difference. Other danger signs include a defensive attitude, being overtired, sleeping too much, forgetfulness, not eating well or feeling sad or depressed. We all need to know our limits and do only what we can. It's okay to say no. It's also a good idea to realize that this is simply one season. It is not going to last a lifetime—although the memories may.

Instead of looking at all that is wrong, find one or two positive elements of the gathering that you can be thankful for. One special smile or conversation with a favorite aunt. One favorite food.

I love this story of Van Varner's family Christmas, the year his nephew Kit asked the family guests to dress formally for a Christmas dinner. Van's brother called him from Chicago. "Kit wants me to bring a tuxedo! I won't do it. I haven't worn that thing in years!" Van tells the story:

I belong to a small family: one older brother Ham and his two married sons. Ham and I are always together at Christmas, either with my nephew in central Illinois, or with the other one in Tennessee. This was the Illinois year. I wondered what formal festivity Kit could have in mind.

"Nothing special," Kit said as I arrived and his two small kids swarmed over me in noisy welcome. "Iris and I just figured we'd like to dress for dinner on Christmas Eve. Family only."

My brother glared. He had that what-have-I-done-wrong expression on his face, that exasperated look of I-didn't-raise-my-son-to-put-on-airs-right-here-in-the-middle-of-these-Midwest-cornfields.

On Christmas Eve I dutifully put on my black tie, and when I came into the living room, Iris was quietly lighting candles, a picture of grace in a shimmering blue gown. Kit, in his tuxedo, was finishing with the logs for the fireplace. The children arrived: Katrin smiling, in love with the romance of her red velvet party dress; little Eric in dark blue serge and black bow tie, stoical, yet intrigued.

Then Ham came. He'd brought his formal clothes after all! Automatically, we all stood up. I'd never seen him more handsome, more patriarchal. He had a dignity that I hadn't bothered to find in him for years.

Dignity—that was the key word for our Christmas. No hubbub, no arguments, no loudness. We laughed and reminisced. The kids sat up straight at the table without being told. And after dinner, Ham looked across at his son and said, "It was a good idea, Kit-boy."

Was it the dinner clothes that made our Christmas? No, not the clothes. It was the disciplined effort we made to honor an occasion. I'm not sure all of us recognized it that evening, but we dressed to honor the birthday of Jesus Christ. And you see . . .

I have found that paying respect when respect is due costs little, but its value cannot be calculated.

SIMPLICITY MADE SIMPLE

PUT YOUR IMMEDIATE FAMILY FIRST. It is more important to meet the needs of your spouse and children than to make sure that your grouchy old uncle is happy. Be flexible with your spouse. If you know that your spouse can only handle your family in chunks, give him or her freedom to take a break. My hubby loves to go antiquing. My family knows this as well. When the family get-together gets too close for his comfort, he finds an antique show to attend. When he returns several hours later, he is refreshed. In the meantime, the pressure is off me, and I can relax and really enjoy my family, not worrying about how he's doing.

DON'T TRAVEL OUT OF GUILT. Travel today is simply not fun. Expecting children and seniors to fare well through the stress of security screening, packed airplanes or busy holiday traffic is unrealistic. Don't be afraid to have an honest talk with family far away about how difficult it is for you to make a trip during the holidays. Suggest visiting at a more convenient time.

KEEP KIDS OCCUPIED—whether you are traveling or simply spending the afternoon with nearby family. In *Real Simple* magazine, Cindy Turner of Chino Hills, California, suggests giving each child a roll of quarters. If there is any fighting or complaining, after one warning the offender(s) must deposit a quarter into the piggy bank. When they reach their destination, the kids get to keep the quarters they have left for spending money.

TAKE MENTAL HEALTH BREAKS. Keith Varnum suggests taking strategic time-outs when family times get stressful. He suggests going to the restroom and splashing your face with water. Or going outside for a breath of fresh air. Or taking a short walk and letting nature revive you. Better yet, make yourself look like a real good guy or gal by volunteering to run errands, wash dishes or even empty the trash.

> Father, sometimes loving others seems impossible.
> Yet, in Your wisdom, You ask us to love others
> as we do You. Help me to see Your eyes
> in theirs, and be Your face to them. Amen.

On Guard against Christmas Depression

A man finds joy in giving an apt reply—

and how good is a timely word!

—PROVERBS 15:23

Depression is one of the leading causes of disability year-round, but you don't have to have a full-blown case of clinical depression to have the blues during the Christmas season. The reality is that more people become depressed during the winter holiday season than at any other time. Lack of sunlight, the demands of shopping and preparation, financial limitations, high expectations, memories of loved ones who have died, and lack of sleep and rest all contribute to exacerbating our already overly busy lives.

Sometimes our own frame of mind can be influenced by people around us, and of course vice versa. I have a friend who doesn't come out of her annual holiday slump until at least the end of January. Normally she is a cheery, upbeat person who you would never suspect suffered the blues during the holidays. But she does. She didn't even return a phone call from me for almost two weeks. What's interesting is that she can't explain why she falls into this state of depression. Her life is good. She loves her job. It just happens. I finally got to see her this year at the end of January, and she was only then emerging from her protective cocoon and returning to the real world.

Let's look at some depression issues that apply particularly, but not exclusively, to two groups of people, the old and the young. Simply knowing what to say to someone who is depressed at Christmas can be difficult. We wish we could say the right thing at just the right time, but to do so requires a little knowledge and wisdom first.

LOOKING OUT FOR EACH OTHER

For most of us, gathering with friends and family to celebrate, to reflect on the past and to dream about the future, can be a happy and peaceful time. However, for some it can be a difficult time. The American Association for Geriatric Psychiatry (AAGP) says that older adults may feel more acutely the passing of time, the absence of parents, siblings and friends who have died, and the distance of loved ones who have moved away. Traditional reunions and rituals of the past may no longer be possible in their absence, leaving the holidays devoid of meaning.

That makes sense. Understanding this means that we need to recognize that it is normal to feel reflective or even sad in the face of such losses of family and friends. However, it's critical to differentiate between holiday blues and something more serious. The key is to notice when our senior loved ones continue to experience the "blues" long past the holidays. What seemed like a simple case of sadness may actually be a serious case of depression.

Most of us want to help those who suffer the blues but we don't know how. For starters, think about how words can help lift the spirits of a loved one who is seasonally depressed. First acknowledge that the Christmas holidays can be difficult. It's okay to admit that life is not always as cheery as the holiday advertisements make it appear. Be willing to be vulnerable yourself and discuss your own feelings about a time when you were depressed or blue. It will help the person to know that you do understand how it feels. Encourage him or her to talk about any fond memories. The most important thing you can do is to listen.

Seniors aren't the only ones who can find the holidays more depressing than cheerful. Children too can be affected. Depression runs in families, which means that some children are more vulnerable to depression than others. Dr. Ann Flynn, a psychiatrist who treats children and adolescents, says, "The holidays can make depression better, or they can make it worse, depending on the circumstances the child is in."

> It's okay to admit that life is not always as cheery as the holiday advertisements make it appear.

For a child who has a positive relationship with his or her family members, the Christmas season will enhance that closeness. However, if the holidays are a reminder of what a child has lost through divorce or the death of a parent, they can be more stressful. That makes it very important for the parent or caregiver to be sensitive to what the child is experiencing. The good news is that the holidays are also an opportunity to spend more time with a child. This will boost the child's self-esteem.

It's important to understand that depression in children does not look the same as it does in adults. Depressed children may act withdrawn but are also likely to engage in power struggles over the smallest things. They tend to pick fights at school and make self-deprecatory remarks. Challenging authority, falling grades and striking out at siblings are all signs of possible depression in children. Dr. Flynn's best advice is to use the holidays as an opportunity for intimacy by spending as much time together as possible. She also suggests creating holiday rituals. "Holidays have meaning, and they create symbols that children carry with them through adulthood," she notes.

Sometimes our moods can take a dip immediately after the holidays. "Children" of any age can be let down with the return to normalcy after the climax of the presents, the dinner, the company. This is true even if you've had a great Christmas. Just think about how drastically different your home looks after removing all the holiday decorations. That can cause most of us to feel a bit let down. Then for some people, added factors of fatigue, loneliness and disappointment over unmet holiday expectations can be overwhelming. That's one reason we need to look out for ourselves and each other—guarding one and all against the Christmas-season blues.

As we learn to keep our expectations within reason for the season and plan for rest and relaxation, the Christmas holidays can be a catalyst for improving our mood. I often remind myself to focus on living in the present, because it's easy for me to always be looking forward to the future. Looking back to the past is an even worse habit to develop. Living in the present, not comparing this year with some cloudy memory from the past, and simply enjoying those we love can be the perfect recipe for a Christmas with a lot of heart. That's what Marilyn Morgan King found out one year when she had plenty of reason to be depressed. She and her children found some laughter in the positive attitude that was integral to an old tradition—which is what we'll talk about in Part Two.

Every Christmas, after our family tree trimming, we'd all stand back and admire our work, and then, without fail, someone would say, "It's the prettiest tree we've ever had!" Then we'd all laugh because those words had become a family ritual. In fact, each year the tree did seem prettier than ever before.

But Christmas of 1988 was different. The children were grown.

I was going through a divorce, and our daughter Karen was hospitalized three hundred miles from home. Our oldest son Paul and his family couldn't make it home for the holidays, so my son John, age twenty, and I went to Topeka, Kansas, to be with Karen. It was a somber trip. After attending Christmas Eve services at the hospital, we brought Karen to our motel room where we had a scrawny artificial tree two feet high with a few packages under it. It was a bleak setting, and the only prayer in my heart was, "Please, Lord, just get us through this." I'm sure Karen and John felt the same cold ache.

But then came the moment of grace. John plugged in the little tree, turned off the overhead light and with a sweeping gesture and twinkle in his eye said, "May I present—*da, da da, DA*—the prettiest tree we've ever had!" Suddenly all three of us were laughing and hugging, and hugging and laughing.

As I've said throughout this section, sometimes a good Christmas is just a matter of attitude.

SIMPLICITY MADE SIMPLE

KEEP THE HOLIDAYS POSITIVE. If you are an adult who fights depression over Christmas, do your best to keep your particular holiday demons at bay. This is especially important if you are a parent of a child at risk for depression. Children easily pick up on parental moods. Dr. Kenneth Johnson, a psychiatrist at Columbia St. Mary's in Wisconsin, suggests defining for yourself what the holiday means for you and how you plan to make it a good memory. He says, "There's nothing magical about the holidays. If you don't get along with your sister during the year, you're not going to get along with her during the holidays." If you understand this, you can protect yourself from unrealistic expectations.

ADD A LITTLE LIGHT TO YOUR HOLIDAYS. Those with a case of the wintertime blues may find some relief with light therapy, which is also called phototherapy. You should first consult with your doctor, but most experts recommend ten thousand lux units, which translates into spending thirty to sixty minutes sitting under the light first thing in the morning. A full spectrum light box is the most common form of light therapy for Seasonal Affective Disorder (or SAD). There are many different lamp styles available for purchase from retailers. Simply ask for a ten thousand lux unit and then choose the one that most appropriately fits your needs.

KNOW THE WARNING SIGNS OF DEPRESSION. A person who is sad or anxious around the holidays will still be able to carry on with regular activities. When the holiday season ends, he or she should return to a normal mood. When people continue to suffer with symptoms that interfere with their ability to function daily, they may be clinically depressed. Depression is a medical illness, and it should be evaluated and treated by a professional. When properly evaluated and treated comprehensively, most people recover. If holiday blues last beyond two weeks and include crying spells, sleep problems, feelings of guilt or thoughts of death, seek medical care. Other symptoms include withdrawal from social activities, lack of energy, excessive worrying, inability to concentrate and weight changes. Remember, particularly for older folks, there may be a stigma attached to asking for help with depression or mental illness—or taking medication. Explain that depression is treatable and something that one doesn't have to live with—whether one is thirty, sixty or ninety. Depression is not a natural part of aging.

BE SENSITIVE TO CHILDREN. A child who is depressed needs special consideration regarding his or her schedule. Make necessary accommodations to keep a child as close as possible to the schedule she is accustomed to. Children, in general, need structure, consistency and attention—especially attention that does not involve toys or other material goods.

GET ANOTHER PERSPECTIVE. Sometimes, we simply need to express our feelings and concerns about the holidays. Take the time to talk out things with a friend or family member. An outside perspective might reveal more options than we can see by ourselves. And don't forget to surround yourself with people who make you laugh. Laughter really is the best medicine for a case of the blues.

> Father, teach me to recognize the signs
> of those who need reminders of Your love.
> I know that in lifting others I, too,
> will be in a higher place. Amen.

PART TWO

Chestnuts Roasting: Christmas Traditions

TRADITION! TRADITION! In your mind maybe you can hear Tevya, the father in the musical *Fiddler on the Roof*, singing out his fervent belief that traditions helped his community survive and his family stay connected. Without tradition we are rootless, he said.

It's true, for any religious group, but those traditions that ground us can also greatly complicate our celebrations. Let's take a look at the ins and outs of Christmas traditions, those that are clearly religious for Christians and those—like roasting chestnuts—that have just evolved across time. Why have they evolved? Maybe for no other reason than "because we've always done it that way."

There's a Reason
for Rituals

"Commemorate this day, the day you came out of Egypt,

out of the land of slavery, because the Lord brought you

out of it with a mighty hand. . . . On that day tell your son,

'I do this because of what the Lord did for me

when I came out of Egypt.'"

—EXODUS 13: 3, 8

Passover was a holiday designed by God to celebrate Israel's deliverance from Egypt and to remind the people of what God had done for them. Christians have no direct command to celebrate Christ's birth, and yet they do. Today Christmas is an annual reminder of what God has done for us. The traditions surrounding Christmas give Christian families and church communities a special sense of belonging. They tie us together.

Developing personal, family and church-community traditions to highlight the religious significance of Christmas serves as a reminder to our elders and a learning experience for the younger ones. Alma Barkman remembers her preschool children Gae and Glen getting really involved in their tradition of opening the twenty-five "December doors" on an Advent calendar.

Behind each little door marking off the days until Christmas was a tiny picture depicting some aspect of Christ's nativity. Every morning Gae and Glen jostled for the chance to open the day's door and tell me how the picture behind it fit into the Christmas story:

"That's the star that led the wise guys to Baby Jesus."

"That's the angel who singed to the shepherds."

"That's Jesus' mommy. She wears a scarf over her head because it's cold in the barn."

Alma says that though their cute explanations amused her, their squabbling over who opened the day's door started getting out of hand. So she issued an ultimatum: "From now until Christmas, neither of you opens the Advent door if you bicker about it." What's more, she said they'd "lose their turn" if they weren't well behaved during the day. The children's interest in the Advent tradition soon influenced their interaction. Alma was surprised to hear conciliatory remarks from the playroom:

"We've only got a few days left, Glen. I'll share my toys."

"Not many days left, Gae. You can have my cookie."

At the Barkman house, the Advent calendar ritual was bringing peace to the whole family.

But there is more to Christmas tradition than religious observation. . . .

When I was young, my family tradition called upon all the children up to age sixteen to create a skit or play. Immediately following dinner, we went to the basement and prepared for our show. I can't say I remember what the plays were about or what roles I played, but I do remember that they were extravagant. One of my cousins, Miles, would do our faces, sometimes, even making the most incredible masks. It's no wonder that today he works in Hollywood. Of course, he insisted on at least one scary character per play, so he could show off his amazing artistic talents to the max. My older cousin Gary, whom I adored, would roll his eyes at us as if we were too pathetic for words. With a dramatic attitude, I would wave off his disdain and proceed as if I were performing at Radio City Music Hall! This was a very big deal to all of us children—we felt so important and excited that the adults would be giving us their full attention for the performance.

> Family traditions are part of the group identity—they can provide a sense of belonging.

In speaking with my mother now about these productions, she says with a kidding smile, that she was "forced" to endure the width and breadth of our imaginations. Nonetheless, when we returned to the living room for the actual performance, all the adults were in attendance. This was how my family celebrated Christmas. It was just part of what gave us a group identity and made us who we were.

In the *Journal of Family Psychology*, Barbara H. Fiese summarized fifty years of research at Syracuse University regarding family rituals and traditions, noting that their symbolic nature provides a sense of belonging and personal identity—aspects that are important for our health and well-being.

The research also showed that people mentally "replay" the activity to recapture the positive feelings of the experience. If this weren't true, I wouldn't be expounding so exuberantly on my early dramatic efforts with my siblings and cousins.

As a third point, Fiese noted that "rituals and traditions also provide continuity in meaning across generations with the anticipation for repeat performance and an investment that 'this is how our family will continue to be.' When rituals are disrupted, there is a threat to group cohesion."

TRADITIONS GIVE US STABILITY

Family traditions can provide the sense of togetherness we all yearn for, especially during the holiday season. In addition, traditions strengthen family relationships and provide emotional stability while maintaining family contact. Traditions also are a wonderful opportunity for helping us remember who we are.

Anna Stewart told *Inspired Parenting* (December 2001): "When I was a kid, on Christmas morning, we would all line up on the stairs and go down together. When I returned one year after I had been an adult for a long time, my three siblings and I still insisted on 'calling' our place on the stairs and giggled like little kids. We felt silly, but it was the right thing for us to do."

When a Web site, christianteens.about.com, asked teenagers their opinions about traditions, they responded positively. One contributor, teen Aaron Cobb, wrote, "These traditions have added continuity to my life—connecting the person who I have become throughout the years with the Aaron of yesteryear. They have added consistency to my life—drawing me back to the truly important aspects of life every year—without fail. They have added coherence to my life—giving me vision for the future and the life that is in store."

As Aaron implies, traditions draw us not only to our families but to ourselves. They can be very personal—something we do alone, for our own seasonal stability. This is what I do because I'm Sharon. This is what I do because I'm a Christian.

As important as traditions are, they don't have to be complicated. Fay Angus says that years ago her family adopted the custom of adding figurines to the home crèche that represent their beloved but deceased pets. A German shepherd, a guinea pig, a kitten—all worship the Christ Child and memorialize their beloved furry friends.

A simple addition to the Nativity symbolized to the Angus family that they were *all* worshiping Jesus.

SIMPLICITY MADE SIMPLE

THINK ABOUT WHICH COMMUNITY, FAMILY OR PERSONAL TRADITIONS ARE IMPOR-TANT TO *YOU*. (In the next chapter we'll delve deeper into traditions that may be important to your family.) Try to finish these sentences:

Christmas wouldn't be Christmas if I didn't . . .

Christmas wouldn't be Christmas if I didn't do . . . with . . . (name(s) of individuals)

Christmas wouldn't be Christmas if I didn't . . . for . . . (names or organizations)

THINK OF ONE CHILDHOOD CHRISTMAS MEMORY that you replay in your mind. It might be eating a certain food, playing a certain game, reading a certain story, acting out a dramatic production. Allow that memory to lighten your load this Christmas season. Does it need to become part of your celebration this year? If making a snow angel on Christmas Eve afternoon will simplify your life—hey, go for it!

BEING ENERGIZED BY AN OLD RITUAL might require cooperation from your extended family. An old tradition that my family revived this year was the sharing of the Oplatek on *Wigilia* (Christmas Eve). The sacred white wafers (much like those used for Holy Communion but larger and rectangular in shape), embossed with a holy picture, are shared with each person present. During the exchange, good wishes are expressed. This is an emotional Christmas moment for a Polish family. This year my family gave me the honor of offering the blessing and beginning the sharing of the Oplatek. It was the first time my husband experienced this tradition, which gives this blessing: *"Na szczescie, na zdrowie z Wigilia!"* (Health and good fortune this Wigilia!) *Abysmy sie doczekali nastepnej Wigilii!* (May we meet next year at this time to celebrate Wigilia!) *Zycze zdrowia, szczescia i fortuny, a po smierci niebieskiej korony!* (May you be blessed with health, good fortune and happiness, which do not tarnish over the years. And may you receive a crown in paradise!) *Niech zawsze nad naszym domem swieci złota gwiazda!* (May a bright star always shine over your home!) *Niech Panna pszeniczna, Betlejemska, zamieni smutek w kolede!* (May the Mother of Bethlehem, the wheaten Maiden change your every sorrow into a carol!) *Niech sie spelnia wszystkie marzenia!* (May all our dreams come true!)

Traditionally Advent is an important season in the Polish year, with special church services, known as Roraty, being held every morning at six o'clock. The four Sundays of Advent are said to represent the four thousand years of waiting for Christ. Simply **SETTING TIME ASIDE EACH WEEK DURING ADVENT TO PRAY** can be a positive tradition.

> Father, You are wise to ask us to pause and
> celebrate religious feasts. As I choose rituals
> to satisfy my desire for a simple Christmas,
> allow me to appreciate them for the stability
> and identity they bring to my life and my family. Amen.

Choosing and Changing
Family Traditions

He who regards one day as special, does so to the Lord. He who
eats meat, eats to the Lord, for he gives thanks to God; and he
who abstains, does so to the Lord and gives thanks to God.

—ROMANS 14:6

As you may know, children (and some adults) can really dig in their heels when it comes to keeping traditions. One night when her daughters were grown, Bonnie Lukes joined them and her grandchildren for a traditional family activity, set in motion decades earlier. Now that she was no longer in charge of the baking, Bonnie felt free to admit her secret: She always hated making cookies. She describes what happened one year, when she decided she really didn't want to give up her "Cookie Night."

I've never been good with dough, and I found the rolling-cutting-sticking-starting-over-again process a maddening one. Every year I wanted to give up. One such year I was attempting (with gritted teeth) to maneuver a

Christmas-shaped tree to the cookie sheet when the girls raced wildly into the kitchen, laughing and pushing and shoving. One of them bounced against me, and the point of the Christmas tree broke off. That was it! My temper flared. "Time out!" I screamed, slamming down the dough. "To the couch right now. And forget about these cookies!" The girls scurried to the couch, and their laughter turned to silence.

Slumped at the kitchen table, staring at my dough-covered fingers, I heard them whispering. "Does she really mean it about the cookies?"

"I don't think so," came the tearful answer. "It wouldn't be Christmas in our house without our cookies!"

The girls were right, I decided. And I scooped up the broken pieces and began kneading the dough into a new ball. What was important became apparent: *"Cookie Night" wasn't about making cookies—it was about preparing for Christmas in our own special way.*

"Girls," I said, "come back and help me. You know I can't make these Christmas cookies without you."

Thus, in our household, an important tradition has continued through the years.

The main importance of traditions is that they create a sense of comfort and security, as did the cookie tradition for Bonnie Lukes' daughters. Some traditions are definitely worth fighting for. But sometimes we simply have to ask ourselves why we do the things we do. For example, I think it would be silly for my family to participate in an old Polish tradition that required hay to be scattered on the bare tabletop before it was covered with a tablecloth. Unmarried girls were to draw blades of hay from under the tablecloth to see what their marital prospects might be. A green strand meant a girl would be wedded quite soon, possibly during the forthcoming pre-Lenten season. A golden blade meant the girl would eventually get married but would have to wait patiently. But a dried and withered strand foretold of a life of spinsterhood. Talk about getting the short straw!

When we question traditions, we develop a greater understanding of ourselves and our family's values. I think there are seasons and transition times in life when it makes sense to change or alter traditions to better suit our current situations.

That said, because traditions are so important and ingrained in our celebrations, we should never attempt to make such changes without consulting those involved. A meeting for all family members to discuss how the family does and will celebrate the Christmas holidays is an excellent opportunity to get everyone talking and opening up about their *expectations, hopes* and *fears*. Are they afraid of change? Are they hoping for a better celebration than last year? What is working? What isn't working—for each person? Just because you have always been the cookie maker doesn't mean that Christmas will be ruined if you pass the rolling pin on to your granddaughter who inherited your baking savvy. In fact, this right of passage can be considered an honor and a new tradition in itself.

It's amazing what you can learn once you get the family talking. You may find that the big extravaganza you are planning really doesn't matter as much as you think it does to the people who love you. Or you may learn that something that is effortless on your part is what your family is hoping to experience during the holiday.

Even the most cherished traditions can sometimes, due to circumstances or limitations of time, lose their shine and get a little lackluster. When they do, don't be afraid to give them some sprucing up.

This is especially critical when there has been a change in the status of the

> There are times in life when it makes sense to change or alter traditions to better suit our current situations.

family. The year my dad died, we all wondered how Mom would respond to our family's traditional Christmas celebration. Rather than guess, we simply asked her. We found that my father's seven-year illness had dampened too many holidays already.

She had done her grieving over the long years of his illness and was ready to "celebrate life" again. Another woman I know was widowed shortly before Christmas. She was not ready to celebrate. Instead, she needed time and a simpler, less involved Christmas celebration. She was grateful when I suggested she discuss this with her children.

> By focusing on simpler traditions, you can slow down and enjoy those things that are most important to all.

Another indicator that change may be the right choice? Does your Christmas season feel like you are running on "fast-forward"? If so, consider creating a newer, simpler version of old traditions to slow down things. By focusing on simpler traditions, you can slow down the Christmas blur and truly enjoy those things that are most important to all. It is only when you punctuate what is important that others will take notice the way they should. After the birth of their first child, one young family decided to start a "new tradition," resurrected from the husband's childhood. Together they read *The Polar Express* to their son on Christmas Eve.

Remember, too, to keep children involved. To keep presents from becoming the focal point of Christmas Day, consider a new tradition scheduled to take place after all the gifts have been opened. Children need some way to occupy that time. One family started a ritual of decorating a tree for wild birds. They placed the tree outdoors close to a window so all the children could watch, and the birds enjoyed their special treat. They used unsalted peanuts in shells, strung with heavy-duty thread, apple pieces, beef suet, peanut butter dipped bread crumbs, rice cakes and popcorn.

One family that couldn't afford to give gifts to everyone chose instead to create prayer calendars. Friends get a "day of prayer" and a copy of the calendar. Every night the family prays for the person of the day.

Rev. Laurie Sue Brockway of New York City and her sisters have started a new tradition especially for their mother, who didn't want them to buy her any more stuff. Last year they filled a pretty container with thank-you notes from her grandchildren, great-grandchildren and assorted in-laws. She loved it so much that they are going to do something similar again this year.

Dream a little. You might be surprised at the results. Most of us spend too much time trying to make Christmas resemble something from the idealized past. Perhaps it is time to initiate a new way to celebrate. One family, at Grandma's suggestion, chose to rent a beach house together. Instead of slaving in the kitchen while bored teenagers complained and husbands watched football, she and her whole family had a great time at the beach! Jo Robinson and Jean Coppock Staeheli, authors of *Unplug the Christmas Machine*, suggest that simplifying the celebration does not have to take away any of its value. In fact, they believe that by creating a new vision for holiday celebrations, you help to remove the burden while providing an opportunity for real joy. "Taking the time to create the fantasy is one of the most important steps you can take. Your fantasies can give you a new enthusiasm for Christmas and the sense of direction you need to start building a better celebration."

SIMPLICITY MADE SIMPLE

Don't wait until you fall down from exhaustion to talk about simplifying Christmas. **HOLD A "FAMILY MEETING"** in which you can reprioritize what family members most want. It's a good idea if you and your spouse first discuss with each other what aspects are most important to the two of you. Then help walk each additional member of the family through a process of identifying what he or she sees as a current and important "tradition." A parent needs to lead the way, explaining that this year we're simplifying to focus on the most meaningful aspects of Christmas.

Consider ideas for working with children—encouraging them to be "big" and to leave behind some of their infantile and labor-intensive traditions. Perhaps if your children are now teenagers or older, you could choose to exchange only a few small gifts rather than continue the frenzy of gift buying. Young children may have celebrated by having a "Birthday Party for Jesus." **AS CHILDREN MATURE, IT'S NATURAL TO MOVE ON.**

To refocus the attention on the Spirit of *Christ* in Christmas, consider establishing **A SPECIAL NIGHTLY DEVOTION** just for the Christmas season. Including spiritual traditions will bring your family closer to God. Some of the simplest acts include praying together, attending services together and reading sacred writings or Bible stories together. One couple chose to create a giant nativity scene on a table. They even gathered moss and real stones from outside to help build it.

REACH OUT TO YOUR COMMUNITY with new traditions. It's easy to become so focused on ourselves that we forget the real message of Christmas. Consider inviting your neighbors over a for a Sunday afternoon Christmas tea to share in your joy and celebration. Another way to make a positive effect on many is through Operation Christmas Child. It's part of Franklin Graham's Samaritan Purse effort, where shoeboxes of gifts are placed into the hands of needy children. This is an especially good way to encourage your children to take the initiative and fill a box on their own. Children love traditions, and this is a significant way of creating a giving tradition.

CONSIDER TRYING SOMETHING NEW THIS YEAR AND SEE IF YOU LIKE IT as a tradition. No one says you can't change it again next year. Remember, the whole idea of traditions is for a sense of community, comfort and security. If your old traditions are creating stress, frustration and arguments among family members, it's definitely time to rethink them. Simply "digging in your heels" to keep things the same may, sadly, leave you alone with your old traditions.

> Father, our traditions will be remembered
> by our young ones and may be passed
> on to and even examined by generations to come.
> Help me to establish holiday rituals that
> will always point to our love for You. Amen.

Transitions and Traditions: When Two Families Merge

"Your people will be my people and your God my God."

—RUTH 1:16

Ruth's promise to her mother-in-law Naomi is often read at weddings. The passage says to the world, "Your family is becoming my family." If it is a second wedding for the bride or groom, the new family bonds might involve children and make for what is commonly called a blended family.

Do you remember Ruth's story? She was not only a widow, but also a Moabite, a different tribe than Naomi's, and Ruth was raised with a different belief system too. But she chose to identify with her mother-in-law, and by doing so she also identified herself with God's covenanted people. Through alliance with His people, Ruth established her claim to a relationship with God.

Eventually Ruth was blessed for her loyalty to her new family with marriage to Boaz. Ruth asked Boaz to cover her with his cloak—symbolizing the protection of marriage. Ruth's faith in the Lord made it possible for her to be an ancestor of David and, eventually, the Messiah. When God chose to work through a Moabitess (Ruth), He showed that the new covenant would be for all people who believed, not just for the Hebrew people.

> When circumstances change, use the opportunity to create new traditions.

Ruth's story is a wonderful example of how blended families should work. Combining families—with or without children—necessitates combining lifestyles. In the midst of all the joy of the marriage, creating a new home involves compromise and even some personal losses, especially concerning highly esteemed traditions. Just as Ruth had to let go of her past traditions in order to become part of Naomi's family, blended families need to let go of some past traditions in order to create cohesiveness within the new family unit.

For newlyweds, remember this: The last thing you want to remember about your first Christmas together is a big fight! Instead, consider mixing a little of your spouse's tradition along with yours. Just because your family has always done it a certain way doesn't mean it's the only way. In fact, any time circumstances change, you have the opportunity to keep some of the old traditions and make new ones. Remember that the holiday is just as important to your spouse as it is to you. Be willing to swap around; for example, you might commit to visiting your out-of-town family the following year while agreeing to stay in town to visit the in-laws this year. This is what my husband and I do.

One of the most important things to remember during your first few holidays together is that you are *married* now. You have your own family—you and your spouse. It's time for you to make your decisions together as a couple and to stand firm. Don't let a well-meaning member of your extended family throw you off by giving you a guilt trip.

If there are children involved in this new marriage, the process of creating new customs can be difficult for kids who have already relinquished their original idea of family tradition when their parents divorced or possibly one died. They then reestablished themselves with one parent, adjusting to a new landscape. Now a new marriage creates yet another set of family traditions. Despite the happiness of new relationships, a former and familiar way of life is lost.

Parents cannot expect their children to simply be grateful for a new two-parent family. Taube S. Kaufman, author of *The Combined Family* and a licensed clinical social worker, explains children's ambivalence: "If children have experienced the death of a parent, they know that nothing lasts forever, and if they have lived through divorce, they know that if one marriage can end, so can another. And, if they trust, and are disappointed again, could they bear the pain?"

Nearly everyone knows a blended family that is trying to form its new family unit. The first few Christmas seasons for stepfamilies will be the most difficult simply because, in the beginning, the combined families might not look or feel like a "real" family. And that is okay—because the truth is that new family members do not share a common history or a mutual definition of how families interact. In fact, the first few holidays may be a disaster, where most of the family is simply relieved when the entire event is over. Some families try to be so inclusive that the children end up with three turkeys to eat at Thanksgiving, and six different homes to visit over Christmas. It's exhausting!

MAKE ROOM IN YOUR HEART FOR CHANGE

Despite our best efforts, this expectation for family togetherness cannot be met by the new configuration of stepfamilies. At Christmastime many children will be reminded anew of the loss of their biological family unit. They may also have conflicting feelings about the creation of this new family. Even the parents may face the pain of change when they have to "share" their children during the holiday school break or even on Christmas itself. As a result, the holidays may produce more melancholy and less cheer than any other season. Acknowledging this reality is important for keeping expectations real.

It's easy to see how disagreements can arise as family celebrations bring ex-family members face to face with their worst fears. Finding a balance within the new family is critical not only for holiday seasons but also for the future well-being of the new family.

Accepting the fact that most blended families can take seven to eight years to really blend is difficult, but it's reality. That's why it is important to negotiate new family traditions despite the fact that they will require a tremendous amount of give and take. Everyone should anticipate feeling a sense of loss as new ways of celebrating holidays and other important events are established.

> By borrowing from old family traditions and adding new ones, you create a new common experience.

But it will be worth it, because the new set of values and traditions is what will define who you are and what you mean to each other as a new family. By borrowing from the old family patterns and creating new ones, you will build a new alliance—just as Ruth and Naomi did. And it is this new commonality of experience that will allow each member of the family to feel included, to know what to expect from others and to have a sense of history that all can share. Psychologist Patricia Papernow calls this "strengthening of middle ground." I like that expression, because it removes the competition. The strengthening of middle ground will grow over time—and the sense of family will increase.

SIMPLICITY MADE SIMPLE

LEARN TO COMPROMISE DURING TRANSITION TIMES. Whether you are a newlywed, divorced or have just moved into your first apartment, this is a time to hold traditions loosely. Let go of some old ones. Embrace some new. Let's say your husband's family always exchanged gifts on Christmas Eve and your family opened gifts on Christmas morning—and after breakfast. Consider alternating gift times one year to the next. It might be a long-term solution, or one of you might actually decide that the spouse's family tradition eventually feels "good and right."

DEVELOP A SOLID COUPLE BOND. This is one of the most critical areas for the new family. If you are part of a blended family, you will feel the strain of being pulled between your own children and the new ones. It will be hard to remain steadfast and loyal to the needs of children who have already endured such loss and change without compromising your new relationship. Offer your children constant reassurance that they are loved and valued. But also recognize that it is by the strength of your new relationship as a couple that your family stands or falls. Your whole family is depending on this relationship making it.

CREATE A PARENTING COALITION if at all possible. Remarried parents must establish a working relationship with the outside parent to resolve issues and plan holidays. Avoid power struggles to ensure open lines of communication between households, and resist the temptation to recruit children in such a struggle. The survival of the combined family may depend on the ability of the divorced parents (and other "ex" family members) to resolve conflicts and be willing to try to work together for the sake of the children. Because he or she cares for you, it will be difficult for your new spouse to stay out of the "emotional conflict." If you and your ex cannot resolve conflicts, you may find yourself turning to your new spouse for support. That can lead to additional problems and conflicts, which will only compound the challenges of the Christmas celebration.

Be sensitive to your children's needs to be with both of their biological parents. My friend Jan found that the simplest way to solve this dilemma was to invite her ex and his girlfriend to join in their family celebration dinner. She also invited her husband's parents, making it a very large celebration. But by including everyone, it made the holiday less stressful and met most expectations. **ENCOURAGE EXPRESSION OF FEELINGS**. Let the children, grandparents and others share their feelings. Listen sensitively and avoid trying to "fix" emotions.

GIVE YOURSELF TIME TO BECOME A FAMILY. Simply getting married does not make two families become one. Acknowledge the holiday confusion and conflicts. Talk about each other's uncertainties without guilt. Keep your sense of humor and laugh about these situations if you can. When compromises aren't forthcoming, put your marriage first. Accept that finding what works for you and your family takes time and experience. Keeping a focus on the joy of your new marriage enhances your ability to cope. Practice what works, and change what does not.

If you are a newlywed, realize that **THE KEY TO PLANNING IS COMMUNICATION**. Let your spouse voice his or her desires and then express your own. Listen to each other. Don't interrupt or get upset while the other is speaking. Wait your turn and focus on that important word on which every marriage is based: *compromise*. Be willing to give a little.

PLAN AHEAD. You can't avoid the inevitable—so face the fact that the first few Christmas seasons may be difficult. Discuss options and plan in advance by encouraging family members to share their ideas for celebrating. Avoid overcommitment and rise above animosity. Remain calm and level-headed even if challenged! And, most important, enjoy your family's uniqueness. Remember, this is the perfect opportunity to practice love.

> Lord, I am thankful that You adopted me
> into Your family, and taught me new ways
> of living, loving and relating to others.
> Help us continue to expand our family relationships
> to reflect the unity that You want us to have. Amen.

Respecting Traditions
of Other Faiths

"Do not think that I have come to abolish

the Law or the Prophets;

I have not come to abolish them but to fulfill them."

—MATTHEW 5:17

Christ's ethic of love does not abandon the rules but shifts the focus of attention from one's actions to the intentions of the heart. With His sin-free life and sacrificial death, Jesus kept perfectly both the letter and the spirit of the law. Although it is impossible for us to absolutely follow the letter of the law, we can attempt to follow Christ's lead in adhering to the "spirit" of the law in this season when we celebrate His birth and the "peace on earth" that the angels announced in Bethlehem. Shifting our focus to the good intentions behind the kindly acts and the seasonal traditions of others who do not share our beliefs could be a very fine idea for everyone, especially in families with two faiths.

"Holidays are one of the most stressful times for interfaith families. Along with events such as weddings, baby namings and coming-of-age ceremonies, the holidays are the most emotional and tradition-laden times to be navigated," says Joan C. Hawxhurst, editor of *Dovetail*, the national periodical for Jewish-Christian families, in her book *The Interfaith Family Guidebook*. The reason is that both partners have very specific and often deeply held ideas about how a holiday—in this case Christmas and Hanukkah—should be celebrated.

> You can respect each other's beliefs without it becoming a threat to your own faith.

My first husband, to whom I was married for twenty years, was an agnostic. Christmas was difficult for us because it was simply a secular celebration for him. His family used the holiday time as an opportunity for vacationing. As a Christian, Christmas was an especially important religious holiday for me that involved very specific family traditions. We never had children, so I can only imagine how much more complicated things would have been if we did.

As adults we could learn to respect each other's differences without it becoming a threat to my faith. But when interfaith marriages reach the child-bearing years, life gets more difficult. Children ask questions—a lot of questions. In fact, it is their best and favorite activity. If you have not thoroughly thought through what is most important about each of your beliefs and your traditions, you can find yourself blindsided by your children's inquiring minds. For children, the various ways their friends celebrate holidays can be confusing. When their parents disagree on certain rituals, they are often left bewildered.

Some people believe that children of interfaith families are more blessed to have the better of two faiths. Others believe that it can bring about a dilution of both faiths, leaving a child with nothing of substance. I will not pretend to know who is right, but I hope to offer some insight into celebrating the holidays in an interfaith family.

Mary Helene Rosenbaum, coauthor of *Celebrating Our Differences: Living Two Faiths in One Marriage*, suggests that the difficulty interfaith couples have with the winter holidays often "really has to do with defining what parts of the celebrations are actually religious and which are cultural and nostalgic." We can waste a lot of time and effort arguing over insignificant symbols or traditions that do not have a foundation in or any influence over our sacred beliefs. By taking the time to identify how we see each of these traditions and symbols, we can focus on what is most essential. When making choices, it is important that both you and your spouse feel that your special holiday has been celebrated properly. As a sign of respect, make every effort to participate in each other's celebrations. By discovering aspects of the holidays that you both enjoy, you'll find that the entire family can celebrate together. This creates a strong sense of unity rather than division.

WEAVE A FAMILY TAPESTRY OF FAITH

It is important to keep the celebration within a comfort level that is compatible with the other's religion. For example, if your husband is Jewish, he may feel that having a Christmas tree or manger in his home is a betrayal of his own religion. One woman found a solution to this dilemma that evolved over fifteen years. She sees three threads that weave together to form what she feels is a beautiful, comforting and inspirational blanket that wraps together and warms her whole family during the winter holidays.

One thread is Hanukkah with its uplifting themes of freedom, miracles and faithfulness to one's values in the face of opposition. The second thread is Christmas, which leads to thoughts of how Christ is present in the world today, what it means to be human, and how we can work for peace and goodwill toward all. The third and final thread of this family "blanket" is all the secular influences of the season, which create fond childhood memories for her children. But she is clear not to confuse the secular with the religious. She doesn't want her children's religious beliefs reduced to or mistaken for the secular symbols.

Hawxhurst says parents in interfaith families should prepare for the winter holidays by explaining to the children how a family's actions and observations of Christmas and Hanukkah complement each other. David Heller, author of *Talking to Your Child about God: A Book for Families of All Faiths,* offers what he holds to be the most crucial element in interfaith parenting: "You and your spouse must believe in your compatibility and in your harmony with God. And you should convey these ideas to your child. There is nothing more reassuring for an interfaith child than a solid and meaningful parental relationship."

In other words, you must know what you believe in and follow through on it in what you do. Interfaith couples must do some serious thinking and negotiating to create a family plan for holiday traditions and celebrations that meets the needs of both parents and, more important, provides for the emotional and spiritual well-being of their children. This can be a lifelong process. But so is the walk to maturity. We don't know what kind of bumps in the road we will encounter until we get there. In the meantime, we must agree that loving one another includes being willing to respect others' spiritual beliefs.

SIMPLICITY MADE SIMPLE

ASK FRIENDS AND ACQUAINTANCES of other faiths to explain their holiday traditions to you. Inquiring and respectful listening will not in any way lessen the value of your own beliefs. Your respectful listening may actually increase your stature in their view. Non-Christians will see that you care about them as individuals. Asking and learning about new traditions also applies to Christians who come from ethnic or regional backgrounds that are different from yours. My friend Nancy is Jewish. We have been friends for nearly three decades, and we both believe our individual faiths have strengthened each other's. We have shared Seder with her friends and family. We offer heartfelt wishes and blessings for Christmas and Hanukkah to each other. Simply caring for each other makes it easy to respect the other's faith.

If you are in an interfaith family, **MAKE A DECISION** about the family's religious identity. Most experts agree that the simplest situation for children is for the parents to agree to raise the children in one faith and one set of traditions. That can be easier said than done. What will you do if you later find that you can't live with that decision? Are you willing to renegotiate? Knowing in advance how important this is to you is critical to maintaining your original position.

TRY SOMETHING FROM BOTH HOLIDAYS. There is no one single way to celebrate any holiday. Every family has its unique twist on celebratory traditions—even if everyone in the family is firmly rooted in the same religious tradition. Acknowledging that, work to personalize your traditions. Try buying a Christmas tree and lighting a menorah. Consider trying different approaches until you find a way that makes sense for you and your family. Then make it your tradition—part of what makes you who you are as a family unit.

TALK ABOUT YOUR DIFFERENCES *before* you have children. It's tough enough just making it work between two parents. Spouses who have talked about their religious differences and how to resolve them are better able to handle the demands of the holiday season than those who put it off. The longer you wait, the harder it will be.

USE THE BIRTHDAY PARTY ANALOGY. Just as we celebrate a family member's birthday because it is his or her day, we can celebrate holidays that one family member feels strongly about even if the others do not feel as attached. Several experts say that the best way to introduce the different holidays and celebrations to children is to use this approach: Explain that you are going to help Daddy celebrate his holiday with a Christmas tree—you can have presents, sing carols and decorate the tree—the goal simply being to help Daddy enjoy the day. Then you will do the same for Mommy when it's her holiday. June Horowitz, an associate professor at Boston College's School of Nursing, leads counseling groups and worship for interfaith families. She encourages families to participate in family traditions. "A Jewish child learning about Christmas is not going to change his identity," she says.

FOCUS ON COMMON THEMES. Celebrate similarities rather than focusing on what makes the holiday preferences different. For example, all major religious and cultural holidays have some element of peace, harmony and reconciliation. You can also honor the differences by embracing the common values and how they relate to your family. The ancient tradition of lighting the Hanukkah menorah has relevant lessons for all of us. After the Jews reclaimed the Temple desecrated by the Syrian-Grecian army, they found one day's supply of the ritually pure olive oil. Miraculously that oil burned in the great menorah for eight days, until new oil was ready. Lighting the menorah each night during the eight days of Hanukkah reminds us of this miracle of provision. It's a miracle we can all honor and celebrate.

AVOID BEING COMPETITIVE. This is so important in an interfaith family. Honor your commitment to coordinate and respect the common wishes of both parents—even after their deaths.

INTERFAITH COUPLES: PUT EACH OTHER AND YOUR CHILDREN FIRST when it comes to extended family. You can't blame grandparents for wanting to share their holidays with the grandchildren. However, you must set boundaries and be firm about them. Whatever you and your spouse agree to in terms of holiday celebrations must be respected by your extended family. Be prepared to abandon some traditions in order to accomplish this. Inform your families early on as to the things that you will participate in and those that you will not. Don't give in under pressure. This is your family and your decision. Simply remind your family members that the holidays are a time of peace and harmony and that your goal is to create a positive experience. The best technique for avoiding explosive differences is a lot of communication with a good helping of humor!

> Lord, help me to balance respect for others
> with my deep sense of faith in You.
> Help me to demonstrate through the holidays
> the reality of what I believe in a way that draws others
> to want to know You more. Amen.

Home Alone? Find Comfort in Traditions

Leave me not, neither forsake me,

O God of my salvation. When my father and my mother

forsake me, then the Lord will take me up.

—PSALM 27:9–10 (KJV)

My goddaughter recently moved into her own apartment. I asked her about holiday traditions and their importance to her. She said, sadly, that at this point in her life, none of the old traditions are working for her because her parents are now divorced. If she could have her "dream tradition," it would be her entire family together for the Christmas celebration.

I'm afraid that her "dream tradition" is out of reach, which may also be the case for thousands, even millions, of Americans who find themselves alone as they prepare for and even celebrate Christmas. Maybe their families have "fallen apart," casualties of divorce. Maybe they're singing "I'll be home for Christmas, but only in my dreams," because they are unable to travel to loved ones celebrating at a distance. Maybe they are widowed and newly grieving. The reason doesn't matter. Being alone at Christmastime can be painful.

For someone like my goddaughter, starting out on her own, I would suggest making a conscious effort to "create" your own Christmas. As Evelyn Bence notes in her book *Leaving Home*, "Sooner or later, there comes a December when the luxury of being the recipient of an already made Christmas melts and must be molded into the adventure of making one's own gingerbread and scrounging one's own tree decorations, although not necessarily by or for oneself only."

One year the young Evelyn threw a Christmas party—mostly to distract herself from self-pity. Later she was amazed to hear one couple admit that the party had been the highlight of their holiday season. Evelyn admits, "*I*, the maker of someone's Christmas? I laughed. It was something I hoped to be doing in ten years, but not something I thought I had already done." Sometimes reaching out to establish traditions of your own, on your own, can be exhilarating.

Even as an older woman with grown children, Marilyn Moore discovered the comfort and joy that can be found in establishing new traditions, based on the older ones. She was facing a Christmas alone. "There would be no stockings hung, no oranges in the toes—a tradition in our family from my mother's childhood on a farm," she remembers.

After Mother married my father, she continued the custom and my sisters, brother and I always found oranges in the toes of our Christmas stockings. Somehow Mother kept alive the Christmas wonder of her

> Sooner or later, many people find themselves in a position of having to "create" their own Christmas.

childhood. Later, I would put oranges in my own children's stocking. But now, what would happen to the tradition?

Then when I received the crate of oranges my friend had sent from Florida I got the new idea . . .

For three days and nights I worked on the oranges, slicing them and boiling them with sugar. I sterilized glasses and the steam filled the house and billowed out into the cold winter air. Finally, there lined up on the windowsill, were gleaming glasses filled with marmalade. New gifts and a new tradition!

An empty-nest Christmas for a single mother turned into an opportunity to make oranges into marmalade.

For someone who is alone and also grieving a fresh, major loss, such as a divorce or a spouse or a child lost to death, the long, dark days before Christmas can seem especially bleak when the sights, sounds and aromas churn up reminders of past celebrations with family and friends. If this is your situation, you may be tempted to pull back and let the holidays pass you by. You may decide to drastically change your holiday traditions or decline invitations, thinking it will help you avoid painful memories. That strategy may leave you feeling worse, not better. If you don't find ways to mark the Christmas season, you will likely find yourself feeling sadder and lonelier than ever. Some—maybe not too much but some—outside stimulation has a way of drawing us out of our private griefs.

MAKE SMALL STEPS

Continuing some of your traditions and celebrations can provide comfort and stability in times of loss and even seeming chaos. The Christmas season can generate fond memories if you let it. But if you have suffered the loss of someone in the preceding year, realize ahead of time that the season will now be different. In *Treasures in Darkness*, a book about the loss of her teenaged son, Sharon Betters says the first Christmas after her loss she consciously chose to maintain some Christmas traditions—like decorating the tree—but dropped others, like hosting a big Christmas Eve gathering. She wisely notes that when someone is newly facing grief, the anticipation of a holiday can be "worse than the actual event."

Remember, Christmas is a time of celebration as well as a time of remembering, and that includes grieving. It's not only okay to grieve; it's important to grieve. Ignoring your grief will not make it disappear.

> Give yourself the freedom to feel rather than block difficult emotions.

Give yourself the freedom to feel rather than block difficult emotions. But remember you are in charge—not your emotions. Learn from your feelings, but don't let negative emotions dominate you. As time passes, your pain will soften. Eventually, fond memories will comfort and lift you. Allow the Holy Spirit to help you take the best of the past into a new future.

For most of us, grief lowers our energy level. Therefore, it is important to avoid being overly busy. Practice self-care to enhance your healing process. That means eating healthy foods, getting exercise, resting and talking to someone you trust about your feelings.

Letting friends and family know how you feel and how you are planning to celebrate (or not celebrate) allows them to help you through the season. It also takes the pressure off them. It's hard for friends to know just what to do when someone they love is grieving. By taking the direct approach of communicating with them, you make it easier for yourself and everyone else too.

Give yourself a break and use this time for reflection. While seemingly everyone is racing around the shopping mall and stressing out about spending too much money and not having enough time, you can create a golden opportunity to simply unwind and let the Lord comfort you.

Allow yourself to respond to your own impulses without forcing yourself to do or act in a specific way. In time, you will be able to embrace your new life. John 16:22 says, "Now is your time of grief, but I will see you again and you will rejoice, and no one will take away your joy." Remember, if loved ones "forsake" you, the Lord—Immanuel—is present.

SIMPLICITY MADE SIMPLE

The key to celebrating Christmas without a family member or members of your family is to **PLAN AHEAD**. For example, if your child is going to be away over the holidays, talk to him or her beforehand and figure out when you can celebrate together. If you have recently lost a loved one, talk to friends and family about your feelings and how you want to celebrate, well before the holiday descends on your head and heart.

Consider anticipating spending Christmas Day alone as a time of spiritual and physical retreat. You never know. This could be an opportunity to indulge in a few of your favorite things or to reconnect with God by journaling and praying. Or it may be the right time to do things you haven't had time for in the past, such as starting a new hobby, cooking something new—or an old standby, calling or writing old friends or even reading a good book. But sometime during the day, try to get outdoors for a breath of fresh air. And wish someone—in person or on the phone—a merry Christmas. Some experts suggest making a *"SOLO PARTY EMERGENCY KIT"* filled with your favorite music and holiday treats. Whatever you do, try to intentionally mark the day—not just ignore it.

Being far away from family and friends can make you feel sad or even hurt. Trying to hide your pain by overindulging in food or spending will only make things worse. Don't beat up on yourself about feeling down either. If you need to have a good cry, do it. Then make the decision to get on with the holiday. Don't be afraid to **SET YOUR OWN SCHEDULE**. If you feel as though you need some time alone, take it. If you feel the need for social engagements, then plan for them.

Now is the time to rely on and especially **RELISH SOME OF THE PERSONAL RITUALS** you've established in the past. These may include Christmas traditions that you have enjoyed with yourself, for yourself, maybe a Sunday-before-Christmas cup of tea at a favorite café, a Christmas Eve hot bath before a church service or rereading a particular Christmas story.

Find new ways of celebrating with old traditions. Sometimes the best idea is to **ADAPT TRADITIONS** as a way of remembering a lost loved one through a special holiday ritual, such as crafting a decoration to hang on the tree, buying a memorial plant for the house of worship you attend or cooking and eating one of his or her favorite foods.

GET INVOLVED IN HELPING OTHERS. I know several singles who have made the holidays special for a lot of other people by committing themselves to selfless activities, such as food drives, working at shelters or rescue missions and visiting hospitals and nursing homes. I read about one man who on Christmas morning decided to bake banana nut bread and take it around to all the neighbors whom he didn't know. It was the perfect way to make new friends and lift his spirit at the same time.

CELEBRATE WITH OTHERS WHO ARE NOT WITH FAMILY. That's what I did the first holiday after I was divorced. My single friends and I had a great time planning our celebration and inviting others who also needed to get together with a new "family by choice."

Lord, somewhere in the great design of life,

You decided that it is not good for me to be alone.

Though I am often tempted to hide away,

I will trust that You know what is best, and I will

find someone with whom to celebrate this wonderful

life You have given to me. Amen.

PART THREE

Deck the Halls: Ambiance and Activities

CHRISTMAS IS A WONDERFUL TIME TO CELEBRATE with glitter and self-expression, when we can demonstrate our God-given creativity. Our personal style, whether simple or extravagant, is reflected in the way we decorate and the gifts we offer. In this section, I will give you suggestions and ideas on how to use simple household items to create a festive centerpiece, and I'll show you how staying true to your personal style makes the most memorable Christmas parties. Although Christmas is the perfect time to use our best china and most ambitious recipes, it is also a time to highlight what we love about others. Good memories will return to you throughout the coming years.

Christmas Creativity

So God created man in his own image,

in the image of God he created him. . . .

—GENESIS 1:27

I love knowing that we have been made in the image of the Creator. That means that we humans are different from the animals and all other creation. The fact that man and woman were made in God's image means we share a likeness with the most creative Being ever.

No matter who you are, you have the ability to be creative simply because you are an heir to the God who created all. You have inherited the ability to be creative. Even if you don't think of yourself as a creative person, you have the capacity to learn, to experiment and to create original expressions of your own ideas. And that is good news when it comes to getting ready for the holidays—especially Christmas, with all its potential adornment.

I have found that most people who think they are creative do express themselves artistically. Those who think they are not creative simply write themselves off as hopeless in that area and don't even make an attempt. A few years ago, I was working with the *Later Today Show* on NBC. Jodie Applegate was one of the hosts but she and I hardly ever got to work together because no one thought of her as "creative." Finally one day they let Jodie do a decorating segment with me in which we used multiple layers of stencils to create a mural on a wall. As Jodie patiently and thoughtfully followed my direction, I could tell she was really enjoying the process. We all held our breath when it came time to remove her stencil pattern and reveal her work. The results were amazing! Jodie had painted an absolutely beautiful little pear on a pear tree with perfectly shaded leaves. She was thrilled as she said, "See, I can be creative!" I think all of us can be creative. It's simply a matter of practice and perseverance—and perhaps encouragement too.

> All of us can be creative—it's simply a matter of practice and perseverance.

There is nothing like a handmade effort when it comes to creating a beautiful Christmas for your family, but don't let your lack of confidence hold you back. Whether it's wrapping presents with care, baking cookies or crafting a special gift, your efforts will be appreciated. The key—regardless of your talents and ability—is not to take on a bigger project than you have time for.

The whole point of creativity is to enjoy the process and not just the results. If you hate the process, you will never be able to appreciate the final work. Instead, every time you see it, you will be reminded about what an awful time you had doing it. I read a line once that said the pleasure derived from the process of whatever we do should be as great, if not greater, than the finished product.

I remember many years ago, when I was first learning to knit, I had this not-so-brilliant idea to make as my first project a pair of white knee-high socks. As I struggled to get the stitches even, I spent more time tearing out than knitting. The result was that one-third of the way through the first sock, the yarn was so dirty and raveled that it was pitiful. I hated that sock. If I had been forced to stick it out with that sock, I would never have knitted another thing in my life. The good news is that my mother realized my frustration and suggested another project. This kept me knitting.

Now all of my nieces and nephews have been blessed with many uniquely designed, hand-knit sweaters, simply because I was steered by my mother in a direction that helped me enjoy the process. This year at Christmas, my niece Stephanie showed up for our holiday celebration wearing the sweater-dress, decorated with a big cow on the front, that I made for her as a child! It now fit like a regular sweater, with three-quarter sleeves, rather than a sweater dress. I laughed so hard and was so thrilled at her little surprise!

> The point of creativity is to enjoy the process and not just the results.

Developing creative thinking can be as simple as practicing the process persistently. Even the most gifted artists study their craft. They also do several "rough" renditions of their paintings before beginning on a new piece of canvas. That's why many old masters' paintings continue to be found. They often are discovered on canvases that have been painted over as the artist practiced for a new painting. Creativity for us mere mortals is never effortless. Strong motivation is what gives us the energy necessary to generate original ideas.

EXPLORE YOUR CURIOSITY

The first rule of creativity is to be open to possibility. Most people are far more creative than they give themselves credit for. Johann Wolfgang von Goethe, the German poet, novelist, playwright, philosopher and one of the greatest figures in Western literature, was quoted as saying that if children were allowed to develop naturally from the day of their birth, they would all be pure geniuses.

What all creative processes have in common is tremendous curiosity. Simple curiosity, not innate artistic talent, leads us to being open to truly experiencing the world in all its beauty.

Dr. Gregory Benford, an astrophysicist at the University of California at Irvine, has written more than thirty books of science fiction; he suggests getting creative juices flowing by looking for comparisons where we don't necessarily think there is any basis for similarity. He asks his students, "How is this thing like that thing, and how is it not?" He says creativity is a process of trying to make a connection that you didn't see before—but you have to be open to the possibility of discovery.

Making a connection that she didn't see before is just what Penney Schwab did one year as she assessed her Christmas decorating scheme. She was talking to her sister Amanda, admitting a bit of envy toward "talented people who carry out a Christmas theme." Amanda proposed that her own theme was "Early Attic." Then Penney decided her theme might be considered "Terribly Tacky." You can see this conversation was getting nowhere, but later, Penney said:

> I walked around the house and studied the decorations. The Nativity on the piano was made from cornshucks, not porcelain, but it reminded me of the stable and the humble surroundings of Christ's birth. The cut-tin candleholder came from our church bazaar and shone as brightly as the star over Bethlehem. And the ornate stick-on window Nativity (number seven in a magazine list of "Ten Trashiest Decorations") had stunning colors that brought to mind the rich gifts of the wise men.
>
> Then there was the tree, which even at six feet could barely

contain all the ornaments. We bought the treetop star the Christmas after we married. We were in North Carolina, miles from friends and family. Michael and Rebecca's Sunday-school craft projects adorned the lower branches. Halfway up was the plaster-of-paris bell Patrick made in kindergarten; it hung right above paper decorations made by his three sons.

I didn't need talent or creativity or more money. I didn't even need a theme, because I already had one: Jesus. The ornaments and decorations are merely reminders of Him and His love. I looked over my beautiful Christmas house one more time, then went to the telephone to call Amanda.

SIMPLICITY MADE SIMPLE

Give yourself a break. One of the primary mistakes people make when it comes to creative work is listening to their own voice of judgment. They tell themselves that the work they are doing is not good enough or not creative enough. Another mistake is assuming that there is only one right way to be creative. Just as each of us is unique, so too is the creative process. Creativity is variable. Creativity gives you the **FREEDOM TO DEVELOP YOUR OWN STYLE**—and that is what makes it so cherished.

EVALUATE YOUR HOLIDAY ATMOSPHERE. This is some of the best advice I have ever heard: Instead of waiting until next year to decide what you are going to do and how creative you want to be, do it just before you put away all of this year's holiday glitter. Take a look around your home and begin writing down your thoughts and feelings about your decorations, gift wrapping and whatever else comes to mind. Think about how you would like to create an atmosphere that reflects you and your family during the holidays. Write down your most significant memory from this year. How can you expand on it for next year? What can you do to help get you and your family into the spirit of the season next time around?

KEEP A JOURNAL. Journaling is a great way to reflect on what you liked about past and present holidays and as a guide for building a better one next time. It's also a great place to map out your Christmas plan. Journaling will help you determine where you are willing to invest your energy. In fact, journaling is an act of creativity too. And it can be an amazing gift. Write about happy memories using decorative writing paper and give it as a gift to those who are part of your memories.

Remember, **CREATIVITY HAS NO BOUNDARIES** except your imagination. Your imagination can be stirred by going through magazines, visiting shopping malls and so forth. You simply have to ask yourself what gives you pleasure and how you can apply it creatively to your life. For example, do you like to doodle, draw or make patterns? Is calligraphy or poetry your favorite pastime? How about painting, decorating or growing flowers? Take some time to think about what you enjoy doing. Make a list arranged according to your preferences. Then set a goal to accomplish something beautiful with your own creative style. My friend Jan painted a tiny clay flower pot and tray a beautiful shade of blue. She added a little silver-paint accent. Then she placed a candle inside and tied it with a white bow to which she attached a handwritten tag: "Star Light, Star Bright." It sits on my desk and is a constant reminder of her love. Simple and sweet.

GET ORGANIZED. Nothing stifles creativity faster than chaos. If you can't find what you need easily and quickly when you are in a creative mood, you will soon discover that you have lost the mood while hunting for your paintbrush! Consider setting up a holiday organization center. One client of mine used an old dresser to store all her wrapping paper, ribbon, scissors, cards and other craft items. It made it simple for her to find time to create, because everything she needed was in one place.

Father, as I behold the creative ways in which
You impart good and perfect gifts to us,
I am inspired to use creatively the talents
You have given me. Please bless the work
of my hands that I might reflect Your likeness
as I decorate and make gifts for others
this holiday season. Amen.

The Art of Holiday Décor

The holly's up, the house is all bright,

The tree is ready, The candles alight;

Rejoice and be glad, all children tonight!

—CARL AUGUST PETER CORNELIUS, "DER CHRISTBAUM"

Paging through each special-edition magazine brimming with new ideas for Christmas decorations can take your breath away. Yes, the pictures are dazzling—but interior design photos illustrating holiday décor can also be intimidating and make you feel overwhelmed. As you drag out the old boxes of mismatched and worn ornaments, don't be discouraged. There are a few simple steps to help add some strategic glitter to your holiday habit.

First, decide how much time, effort and money you are willing to spend on decorating for the holidays. Most of us would agree that the less the better, but we also want to be delighted by the beauty of Christmas. One reason for loving the season is that we get to spend more time than normal with family and friends. Finding just the right balance can be as simple as using decorating to encourage togetherness and establishing new traditions while creating special memories by doing some of the decorating together with family and friends.

Second, create a blueprint for your Christmas decorations by deciding whether or not you want to use a theme. Lots of things can inspire a theme. For example, a favorite Scripture, poem or even a Christmas carol can be the spark for all your holiday décor. You can also be inspired by color. In fact, changing your holiday color can make a fabulous difference simply and inexpensively. A few new ribbons, a few new ornaments and natural plant materials can give an otherwise worn collection of decorations a completely different feel. And how it feels is what decorating is all about.

> Decorating creates an atmosphere that invites you to feel good about the season and to recognize what a special time it is.

The whole point of decorating is to create an atmosphere that invites all to feel good about the season and to know that it is a special time. Theme decorating makes the entire process simpler, because it allows you to focus and not be confused by so many options. As most who know me realize, my favorite place is the beach, so despite the fact that I live in a community far from the beach, I use shells as the theme for my holiday decorating scheme. The combination of shells, greens, lights and ribbon makes a festive appearance that announces Christmas in my unique style without breaking the bank.

As I mentioned earlier, I finally gave in and ordered a fine, artificial pre-lit Christmas tree from QVC. Rather than pretending it was like all the real trees of the past, I chose not to use most of my old colored ornaments. Instead, I stuck with my shells and old white ornaments and added large teal and white bows, along with a few new teal ornaments. The tree was beautiful. Almost every time he walked past it, my husband said, "You really outdid yourself this year." Actually, it was one of the easiest trees I've ever decorated. Even undecorating it was simpler than in the past, because the lights did not have to be removed and rewound! I also invested in two new ornament-storage boxes that allow me to leave the wire hangers on the ornaments and shells and simply hang them in the cases, which are padded with foam to keep everything safe and ready for next year. Making these changes was definitely worth it. I thoroughly enjoyed having the tree this year even though we traveled nearly ten days throughout the holiday season. I left the tree up through the first full week of January, not having to worry about a real tree drying out and dropping needles everywhere.

My new artificial tree revitalized my attitude toward Christmas decorating. What will I do with the old ornaments? Eventually they will go to my goddaughter Lexi. This year we got her a little fake tree with a few tiny ornaments—perfect for her small apartment. Eventually Lexi hopes to have a larger apartment in which she can have a bigger tree.

DO WHATEVER YOU CAN DO

Another way to simplify the holiday without diluting it is to choose to focus on doing just one thing exceptionally well. For many people a Christmas tree captures the best of the holiday ambiance. Jo Robinson and Jean Coppock Staeheli, authors of *Unplug the Christmas Machine*, say that the way a tree looks is only part of how people feel about it. "Most people also respond to the sentimental value of familiar ornaments, whether or not they are beautiful. And they tend to get more enjoyment from a tree if they have had a good time decorating it. A tree decorated by one person spending a lot of time will often have a gratifying artistic unity to it, but a tree that involves the whole family is often more satisfying overall."

My friend, author Cris Bolley, reminded me that the reason we decorate is to help set the season apart from the other days—but sometimes it just seems like too much effort. Here's how Cris got her Christmas groove back a few years ago:

In past years, my three daughters helped me decorate the house for Christmas. But as they have grown and moved on, decorating has become less eventful and simply more work for me. Last year, I had only one teenager left at home to decorate with me; but she was too busy to help me, and our nine-foot artificial tree was too heavy for me to handle alone. So I bought a four-foot, pre-lit tree for only twenty dollars and decorated it with all gold ornaments, cards and ribbons and set it in our front living-room window. I also used a fifty-percent-off coupon from the paper to buy an automated sleigh and reindeer to place in our front yard—again, it was something I could put up and plug in by myself since my husband was also losing interest in decorating the roofline with lights. It seemed to him that since the girls were grown, the purpose of decorating the house was losing its "pizzazz."

But once I put up the little tree and the dashing reindeer on the lawn, something amazing happened. Seeing my humble little effort to set the day apart, my teenage daughter insisted on getting the big tree out of the attic. Her boyfriend helped us put it together and we set it in the main entrance by the stairs. And on seeing my little sleigh and reindeer in the front yard, my husband was inspired to put lights on the shrubs and roof again. Soon all the mantels and countertops in the house were graced with pine boughs, lights and ornaments collected from years of merry Christmases.

When my nearly three-year-old granddaughter Riley came to visit us, Grammy's house was full of trees and exciting activity. When she was leaving the house that night she walked up to the reindeer on the lawn and stood motionless as she watched them leaping to take flight into the air. I watched her stand so still, as if afraid to scare them away. I stepped beside her as she stared at the wonder of the dancing deer against the backdrop of tiny lights on the house and trees. Quietly she whispered, "Grammy, can I ride them?"

The decorations had marked the day. . . . Christmas became a day when a little girl believed that anything might be possible. Without the lights and trees, Christmas would have been "just an ordinary day" at Grammy's house.

SIMPLICITY MADE SIMPLE

MAKE DECORATING THE TREE A SPECIAL FAMILY TRADITION. Start by assigning everyone a task and setting aside a whole day for the event. Be sure to reserve certain ornaments for each child to hang. Make the crowning star or angel a privilege for the youngest child to place on top of the tree (with a little help, of course). You could also make this a tree-trimming party and invite the neighbors or extended family. Set the mood with your favorite holiday music and eggnog. Encourage young children to make things to hang on the tree, and be sure to have the family collect ornaments year-round. I always shop for Christmas ornaments on vacation in the summer. Give your child or grandchild an ornament every year—eventually this can become a treasured collection that lasts a lifetime.

MASTER THE ART OF TREE LIGHTING. David Stark, a Brooklyn, New York, floral designer, says the trick to hanging lights on your tree is to go up and down, not around. Start by dividing the tree vertically into three sections and string the lights by sections. Always plug in the lights before you begin, to identify any defective bulbs. Start at the bottom and weave each string in and out of the branches, to the top of the tree and back. David Murbach, manager of the decorators for New York City's Rockefeller Center, says to use the trunk-to-tip method to create "not just a shell of light but an inner glow and a three-dimensionality that cannot be achieved any other way."

The visual appeal of **CANDLELIGHT AND THE WARMTH IT EVOKES** have an undeniable attraction. References to candles date back to the early thirteenth century B.C. in Crete and Egypt. The quality of candlelight depends upon the type of material used. Although beeswax is still considered the best, soy candles are the cleanest burning. And there's a specific height to which a candlewick should be trimmed—one-quarter inch. You can completely avoid those black ugly specks melted into the top of your candle by trimming the wick after each use. To create a very pretty tablescape, combine candles of uniform color in a variety of shapes and widths. For an elegant look try placing different-height tapers in a straight line down the center of your table. Of course never leave a burning candle unattended. Because I have cats, I thought I was smart when I placed a candle high up on a shelf. I then left the room to put on some lipstick. When I returned, the candle had started to burn through the shelf above! Now I usually use the new battery-operated candles. They are made of wax and come in several shapes and sizes. But instead of a flame, they have a flickering light placed deep into the center that operates with a switch on the bottom. I love them!

Indulge your senses. **INCORPORATING SMELL INTO YOUR CHRISTMAS DÉCOR** will make your rooms most pleasing. Scents infuse and transform the season into a magical and unforgettable experience. The alluring aroma of spices and freshly baked goodies, the clean crisp scent of pine needles or the perfume of frankincense and myrrh are sure to put you in a holiday mood. Essential oils are an easy way to add holiday aroma. Homemade potpourri and sachets can be prepared five to six weeks ahead of the holiday season. In a plastic bag, sprinkle essential oil, dried flowers, leaves, nuts, seeds and berries. Or simply place a wreath of silk or dried florals and greens in a bag and scent with a few drops of your favorite essential oil. I love using juniper, cedar wood, spruce and balsam. You can also choose heady scents like myrrh and sandalwood.

MAKE A SPICY-SCENTED TREE ORNAMENT. Here's a simple recipe:

> Combine the following ingredients:
>> 1 cup cinnamon
>> 1 tablespoon cloves
>> 1 tablespoon nutmeg
>> ½ cup applesauce
>> 1 tablespoon sparkle stars
>> 2 tablespoons white glue

> Once combined, roll out as a dough and cut with shaped cookie cutters (stars, snowmen, etc.). Use a straw to make a hole for the ribbon to hang. Dry for three to four days, turning regularly.

Go au naturel. **FRUIT MAKES THE PERFECT HOLIDAY ACCENT** in wreaths, garlands and centerpieces. Deck yours with cloves, ribbon, greenery, tassels and glitter. Real fruit works well for outdoor wreaths. Simply replace as needed. These wreaths can also last for several days indoors—adding a wonderful natural fragrance to your home. You can decorate with pears, apples, pineapple, pomegranates, berries, oranges, lemons, kumquats and sugar plums. To add some festive color to a plain white pillar candle for a centerpiece, set it into a clear glass container, such as a bowl or a hurricane globe, and add mini-limes, rosy crab apples and some cranberries to create the perfect holiday blend. It's elegant, colorful and very easy to make. Wrap a pretty ribbon around the outside of the container and it's dressed for the season.

MAKE YOUR OWN HOLIDAY DECORATIONS. Here are a few simple ideas.

1. Styrofoam balls wrapped in ribbon make a pleasing mantel decoration. Use various sizes and colors and then add a little greenery to complete the look.

2. Clear glass containers filled with holiday twinkle lights create the right atmosphere for adding sparkle to your holiday table or mantel. Or they can be stuffed with treats, such as candy canes, holiday gumdrops or even mints. Add a ribbon, flower or greenery, and you have a beautiful and edible display for all!

3. For a fun and kid-friendly outdoor project that will also benefit the birds, consider making fruity strands and nutty garlands as P. Allen Smith, gardener extraordinaire, did: Simply thread dried apple and orange slices onto lengths of raffia. Cut bread ornaments with circle, star and candy-cane cookie cutters; smear with peanut butter, then dip in birdseed mix. String fresh cranberries onto strands and arrange on branches as you would hang lights on a tree.

4. Keep it simple, year after year, with a basic wreath. When I was a young bride on a very tight budget, a friend made four little wreaths from tiny little pinecones for me. Those wreaths were the basis of my holiday décor for years. I changed the ribbon and included a few additional ornaments and accessories to give them a fresh look each year. You can do the same with a basic grapevine wreath. Add ribbon in your chosen style, whether it's country plaid or fashionable satin for a truly personal touch.

Lord, thank You for making our smallest efforts
seem grand in the eyes of those we love.
Set loose creative ideas in me, so I will learn to use
what I already have in order to
bless people on Your behalf. Amen.

Company's Coming!

Go, eat your food with gladness,

and drink your wine with a joyful heart,

for it is now that God favors what you do.

—ECCLESIASTES 9:7

A few years ago, I was scheduled to be the keynote speaker at a large conference. When I checked in the day before, just to make sure everything was on schedule as planned, I was surprised to find out that somehow the conference brochure had listed me as an "entertaining expert" instead of an interior designer. That gave me exactly twenty-four hours to figure out what to do. As I began thinking about how I entertain, I realized that there is a strong correlation between decorating and entertaining. Just as I suggest that my design clients be true to themselves and their lifestyle in their decorating—the same considerations should be made for entertaining.

When decorating you must consider your family and way of living in a realistic setting; you can't expect to turn country bumpkins into fancy city slickers simply by choosing formal furnishings. If you try, you will be disappointed. There is no rule that says just because it's Christmas, you must have an elaborate sit-down dinner. If you are really a chili person, then don't try to serve a seven-course fancy meal—serve chili out of a sparkling bucket and let everyone come in jeans and be comfortable.

When it comes to Christmas entertaining, choose the right format for your home and your personality.

My hypothesis was confirmed as I began researching this book. I found several books on entertaining written by interior designers. We all had come to the same conclusion. It can be as simple as asking yourself a few key questions, whether you are considering decorating or entertaining: What are your family responsibilities and your lifestyle? How much time do you really have to devote to this project? How much money can you realistically afford to spend? What are your personality strengths and weaknesses? How many people can you, or do you expect to, entertain at once in your home? Ultimately, as the great American decorator Elsie De Wolfe extolled, the hallmarks of good taste are "simplicity and suitability."

When it comes to Christmas entertaining, choose the right format for your home and your personality. If you have a small home, serve buffet style. If you have a small dining room or none at all, set up tables in the living room or family room. If you don't have fancy matching table linens, purchase some inexpensive Christmas fabric and drape it abundantly—allowing it to puddle on the floor; no sewing is required.

SIMPLY ENJOY YOURSELF AND YOUR GUESTS

Ultimately, your goal should be to make sure that you and your guests enjoy each other. Notice that I said you and your guests. Make it easy on yourself—the more

Determine what level of decorating you are willing to keep up with in your home.
A few small touches can be just as inviting as extensive decorations.

Soft candlelight adds
a warm glow to these
simple table centerpieces.

Set aside time each day for joyful worship. It will deepen
the meaning of your Christmas celebration.

These handmade stockings add a personal touch to this mantel's decorations.

For those short on time, decorated gift bags are a terrific alternative to more traditional gift-wrapping.

The most touching gift is a gift from the heart. If baking is your talent,
try sending homemade cookies as a gift.

Choose ornaments
that are meaningful
to you and your family.

Don't feel pressured to do more outdoor decorating than you want to.
The simple wreath and miniature trees shown here convey a sense of celebration.

you enjoy yourself, the more your guests will enjoy themselves. A buffet dinner can be as grand as a formally seated multicourse meal. It's all in your attitude.

If cooking a seven-course meal makes you want to forget dinner all together, then provide the entrée and the beverages and let the guests bring everything else. If your mother-in-law always criticizes your cooking, suggest she bring the entrée and you provide the rest. My family always gets together on Christmas Eve. Each of us is expected to bring something, and the host provides only what she wants to cook. If even this sounds like too much, hire a caterer and enjoy!

Remember that you don't have to do everything yourself. Choose the things you enjoy doing the most and focus on them. Then hire someone to do the rest. Make it a gift to yourself and your family. For example, if cleaning is not where you want to put your effort, then just for the season, hire a cleaning service.

Entertaining is an opportunity to express your ideas of what a party should be rather than following the dictates of any entertaining diva. Remember that this is the season to celebrate. That means it should be fun. Have fun planning your menu. Have fun making your home look and smell inviting. If pulling out your finest china and your best party dress makes you feel good—then do it. And enjoy your time with others, without forgetting the reason for your gathering, as Pam Kidd almost did one year.

> Your goal should be to make sure that you and your guests enjoy each other.

On Christmas morning, long before the sun rises, I set a huge pot of wassail on the back burner of the stove. Soon the house is filled with the smell of oranges and cloves and cinnamon, and a flurry of activity. In an hour, twenty-two people will be arriving for our annual Christmas breakfast, which we have traditionally shared with single friends and those who are lonely or without family near. Son Brock is off across town to pick up Frances Faulkner. Daughter Keri is checking to see that there's a remembrance under the tree for each guest. My husband David is working with my stepfather Herb to set up tables and chairs. My mother, Bebe, and I are working as fast as we can in the kitchen.

Later, seated around our stretched-out table, the faces of the guests blend with those from other years: an old couple who spent their lives as missionaries in China; a family of refugees from Vietnam; a lonely widower; a young family far away from home; a sweet woman, mentally challenged. All sizes, shapes and colors of people have gathered round our Christmas table this year. In their midst, David smiles, Bebe and Herb chat happily. I see Keri reaching over to hug ninety-one-year-old Frances, and Brock refilling wassail cups.

Then I see that in the rush I have forgotten to light the candles of the Christmas carousel in the center of the table. When I do so, the shepherds and wise men take up their journey, and the candlelight flickers on the faces of the guests. I smile in recognition: The Light, which enlightens everyone, has come. Christmas is here!

SIMPLICITY MADE SIMPLE

CREATE LASTING MEMORIES. A special party is unforgettable; its memory may well outlast any gifts exchanged that year. The basics for any party are the same—but it's how you customize the details that makes the difference. Think in terms of hospitality rather than making the social grade. Dress up your table with your favorite serving dishes. Consider using that heirloom silver and pretty porcelain you've been saving. If you don't have any—then invest in simple white platters. They can be found almost anywhere and are elegant and inexpensive. Measure your success by how heartily your guests eat, laugh and talk.

SIMPLE CAN BE EXTRAVAGANT. Serve comfort food. Start by deciding what kind of menu you want as far ahead as possible. One of my favorite holiday meals is a standing rib roast served with my version of Yorkshire pudding. I make the pudding in muffin tins. It never fails and makes serving so much easier. Always include some healthy, low-calorie selections. Try serving something unusual when it comes to vegetables. My new mashed favorite is cauliflower. Serve it as you would mashed potatoes. Prepare and freeze whatever you can in advance.

Don't feel as though you have to make everything from scratch. **ORDER SPECIALTY ITEMS** or even dessert from your favorite bakery. Working at QVC has a lot of advantages. This year, I discovered how amazing their food selection is. I ordered barbecued ribs that I simply had to heat and eat! Of course there are lots of companies from whom you can order some or all of your meal. It may be a bit more expensive than homemade, but it sure is quicker, and sometimes that is worth the money.

FOR A BUFFET-STYLE MEAL, avoid anything that can spoil when left out for hours. One of my favorite wintertime buffet meals is a large pot of chili, a large pot of Hungarian goulash, several hearty breads and a variety of cheeses. Because I live in the Northeast where it's plenty chilly in winter, I can make my soup and goulash the day before and leave it on the back porch to keep cold. Then the evening of the party I simply bring in the pots and place them on the stove, where my guests can serve themselves right from the pots. I purposely purchased some very pretty ladles to make it more festive. I also am sure to place hors d'oeuvres throughout the living, dining and kitchen areas so that no single room gets too crowded. I place a beverage station on the back porch (to keep cold drinks cold) and another hot-drink station in the kitchen. I place a basket of wrapped flatware in each room for easy reaching. For dessert, my favorite is Mrs. Prindle's caramel and nut-covered apples.

Plan your table. I always set my table the day before. It's something my mother did— so I guess it just stuck with me. I love dressing the table—it is one of the more relaxing things for me to do. A tablescape, kind of like a landscape, is a great way to **MAKE A TABLE SPECIAL.** It's also a fun way to make a unique statement and is enjoyable to plan. Consider combining the color(s) you used throughout the house for your napkins, tablecloth, placemats and centerpiece. I love to incorporate candles into my centerpiece as well as greenery, berries, fruits or shells. But use whatever appeals to you. One year I used fresh vegetables and shined them with oil. Another year I used pebbles and candles. Allow yourself to simply have fun.

MAKE A MASTER LIST of what must be done one month, one week and one day in advance. Be sure to plan your seating arrangement too. This is especially helpful in keeping old family rivalries from being revived. Place talkers with nontalkers to keep the conversation lively. Be sure to inquire if anyone has any special dietary needs or food allergies. Choose recipes that are familiar to you and do not require you to spend a lot of time in the kitchen. Your guests will begin to feel guilty if you do. Do as much of your shopping as you can two weeks ahead— leaving only those things that cannot be done in advance for the last minute.

ENLIST HELP. Consider ways to give children ownership of the gathering. This can make them feel important and ease your workload. If you're having a sit-down dinner, they might make place cards and help set the table. If it's a buffet, they can wrap settings of flatware inside dinner napkins. During the gathering, children might also greet guests at the door, handle their coats, and introduce anyone new to the rest of the group.

SAYING THANK YOU. You might assign a couple of children to be official photographers at the gathering. Then create a collage of photos along with a "thank you for coming" letter to send to all your guests. It's a great way to keep the holiday spirit.

Remember, your **GUESTS SHOULD BE THE FOCUS**. The goal of a Christmas gathering should be to put everyone in a festive mood that will set the tone for the coming year.

> Lord, it seems that the years are remembered only
> by these special days that we set aside
> for each other. Thank You for giving us reason
> to celebrate, and for filling our tables
> with more than enough for everyone. Amen.

Making and Baking: Are We Having Fun?

But Martha was distracted by all the preparations
that had to be made. She came to him and asked,
"Lord, don't you care that my sister has left me to do
the work by myself? Tell her to help me!"

—LUKE 10:40

It's amazing the difference an attitude can make. Holiday preparations can be a drag, or they can be a wonderful time for family fun and bonding. It's all in how you see it. When I think about the Christmases past, it astonishes me that many of the best times were actually about preparing food that involved a lot of work. At Easter, every year, my family makes fresh kielbasa from scratch with Great-grandma's old sausage stuffer. Even the men get involved as they gently coax the skins open so that the women can fill them.

From as far back as I can remember, Mom baked cookies at Christmas. I don't mean a few dozen—I mean enough cookies to last two or three months for a family of eight! Mom has several old and very large lidded crocks. As the cookies cooled, they were placed gently into the crocks for storing. The crocks of cookies were kept in our outer foyer—where it was as cold as a refrigerator—or colder, depending on the Cleveland winter. Baking cookies was something that we children were encouraged to participate in. Thumbprint cookies were always a favorite. After all, what could be more fun than sticking your pudgy little thumb into cookie dough?! *Mmm, mmm*, good.

When I called my sister Wendy, who is ten years younger, and asked her what the most significant holiday activity is for her, she responded without hesitation—"Baking cookies!" And her favorite cookies are "thumbprints and kolachi." Kolachi are a traditional Polish cookie that can be filled with almost any kind of fruit preserve. Today, our family Christmas cookie-baking tradition continues and now includes a younger generation whose own children will soon be adding their chubby little thumbprints to the cookies. This year my family spent two ten-hour days baking cookies! Now that's what I consider a gift.

WORKING TOGETHER BONDS US TOGETHER

The *Lancaster New Era* (March 7, 2005) reported on one local family that sees crafts as their holiday bonding time. There is a sense of family togetherness as the parents help their children, ages four and six, weave pipe cleaners through felt to build wiggly inchworms. Crafts, from cross-stitch to homemade Christmas ornaments, help keep this family close. "Crafts are a pretty big thing in our home," says Mom. "It's time spent together. Not just staring at the TV and not saying anything—it's actually learning something and actually interacting. It also gives the children a sense of accomplishment," she says.

The same article noted that Terry Ouellete, a national spokeswoman for the nonprofit Craft and Hobby Association, says the number one reason people do crafts is to make gifts for someone. That makes crafting a nearly perfect holiday activity. It's a chance for family team-building and an opportunity to create one-of-a-kind gifts for those you love.

Family projects aren't always perfect, but that doesn't matter because what you are really looking for is a chance to create memories. One mom created memories for her and her five-year-old son by decorating a ginger-bread house using a kit from the bakery, which included frosting and colorful candies such as gumdrops. You could even create an entire village by using different candies on each house. Set the scene with coconut or granulated sugar as a snowy base. Then place the houses on cake stands to vary the heights. Tin foil, flattened out smoothly, makes a fine skating pond. My friend Michelle has kept her daughter's gingerbread houses from the past several years. It's so much fun to see how her talent has matured!

> Making holiday crafts provides a perfect opportunity for family team-building.

Be brave and experiment to create a unique Christmas atmosphere each year with and for your family. By doing so, you encourage creativity while dressing up the house. Something as simple as customizing store-bought photo albums by glu-ing sheer glimmery fabrics over the covers and finishing with a seasonal picture can be the perfect gift for grandparents or friends.

When I was very young, my mother taught me to knit—an ageless craft. Grandmothers and children alike can work side by side to knit some of the best gifts ever. Garter-stitch scarves, made throughout the year, can be personalized by embroidering the recipient's initials or a holiday motif in a contrasting color yarn. If even this doesn't sound simple enough, then buy one-color scarves and add your own personal decorative touch. The results will still be handcrafted and heartfelt.

Keep things simple. Start by changing your attitude; just because it's Christmas doesn't mean you have to go beyond what you are comfortable with. If baking twenty different kinds of cookies is not your cup of tea, then make a ton of plain sugar cookies and cover them with lots of decorations. Make it a family event. Fill the table with frosting, brightly colored sugars, sprinkles, crushed candy canes and let your decorating team have free rein! Later serve the cookies for dessert. It's not a lot of effort, but it makes things fun.

SIMPLICITY MADE SIMPLE

Remember, it's the simple things that usually mean the most. Just as our family's fondest joy is baking lots and lots of cookies together, you too can find great joy in a simple activity as long as it involves the people you love. One idea that not only benefits those less fortunate than ourselves, but also helps clean out the clutter is to take the time after opening your presents to **PUT TOGETHER A BASKET OF GOOD STUFF** you no longer need to give to a charitable organization. For example, whenever I get a new pair of shoes, I choose a pair to donate to poor families in Jamaica. You can do the same as you put away your new stash of holiday treasures. Or you can also take up the British tradition of Boxing Day, which falls on the first weekday after Christmas—usually December 26—and coincides with the Feast of Saint Stephen. There are conflicting stories of what the term Boxing Day means, but one tradition says that in Victorian England, the poor went from house to house bearing boxes that compassionate homeowners filled with food, clothing and gifts.

MAKE THINGS IN MULTIPLES. Big-batch baking or cooking is the perfect family holiday activity. Whether it's soup, stew or lemon pound cake, this is a great way to get some of the holiday preparations done while having a blast. Put on your favorite holiday music and sing while you work. One family of sisters watched their favorite holiday movie while baking and cooking. They laughed. They cried. They danced. They loved!

If your family is the outdoors type, capture the spirit of the season together by **FORAGING IN THE WOODS** for scraps and souvenirs that you can use to create your holiday décor. With a little ingenuity, you can find armsful of treasures in twigs, vines and moss for weaving around the base of candles on your table. Humble twigs can become enchanted when they are crafted to create a crown of stars for your treetop. A single large pinecone adorned with a glass bead and ribbon glued to the top becomes a jewel of an ornament. Tallow berries wired with a garnish of baby's breath can create a simple but elegant napkin ring. Remember that when crafting with nature, a little goes a long way. For example, a miniature star fashioned from a birch twig provides an element of surprise and draws attention.

Recapture the Christmas spirit by **PLAYING GAMES WITH CHILDREN**. Their innocent sense of celebration is contagious. Allow yourself the freedom to act like a child. Laugh at yourself and invest your energy in something totally playful. Try seeing Christmas through the eyes of a child. Look for the magic and the miraculous. Take time to relish the sounds, sensations, sights, tastes and smells of Christmastime.

Reminisce. **BRING OUT OLD PHOTOS THAT EVOKE HAPPY TIMES**. It's a fine way to keep family history alive and relevant. You may even want to incorporate photos into your decorating. It's a great technique for inspiring a sense of importance within the family. Record your memories and create new traditions. As your family gathers around the dinner table, use this time to make plans for next year. One idea could be to plan to offer a collective hand, together as a family, within your community. Ask everyone to volunteer ideas about where and how to help.

Honor those no longer with you by **USING TIME-TESTED FAMILY RECIPES** as part of your celebration. Kolachi cookies have a long history in my family that goes back generations. But the "secret" recipe has been guarded and never shared with anyone who was not related to us.

> Lord, thank You for the family and loved ones
> with whom I work and play during my
> Christmas season. We know that activities can
> energize us or drain us. Give us Your grace
> to choose our family activities wisely, so that
> we are showing honor to You. Amen.

Join the Chorus

Adeste, fideles, laeti triumphantes;

Venite, venite in Bethlehem.

Natum videte Regem angelorum.

    Venite adoremus,

    Venite adoremus,

    Venite adoremus, Dominum.

O come, all ye faithful, joyful and triumphant,

O Come ye, O come ye, to Bethlehem.

Come and behold Him, born the King of angels;

    O come, let us adore Him,

    O come, let us adore Him,

    O come, let us adore Him, Christ the Lord.

—JOHN FRANCIS WADE (1751)
TRANSLATED BY FREDERICK OAKELEY (1841)

As I mentioned at the beginning of this book, singing Christmas carols in Latin when I was a child set them apart for me as special. "O Come All Ye Faithful" is one of my favorites. Every time I hear this carol I still find myself singing in Latin rather than English.

The story of Jesus' birth has inspired composers for more than two thousand years as they strive to recreate the song of the angels singing at the arrival of the Messiah. I cannot even imagine how beautiful that sound must have been. Yet even more beautiful is the grace-filled gift that God gave us through the birth of His Son.

George Frederick Handel's *Messiah* is one of the most popular pieces of choral music ever composed. For some, the uplifting choruses, "For unto Us a Child Is Born" and "Hallelujah!" are practically synonymous with the Christmas spirit.

An impoverished, aging composer, Handel was asked to write the music for the *Messiah* oratorio for a charity group in Dublin, where it was first performed as a benefit concert in April 1742. Handel even conducted the opening perform-ances, with the choral parts sung by community amateurs. The work's familiar biblical text and the music's grand accessibility drew crowds, making the produc-tion a success, eventually all across Europe. Traditionally audience members stand up at the "Hallelujah Chorus." But do you know why? We're following the lead of the king of England, who showed his respect for the higher "King of kings" and "Lord of lords." Back then, when the king stood, everyone in the audience followed suit!

CHRISTMAS IS A TIME FOR SINGING

One of the oldest holiday activities is caroling. Caroling has a lively and varied his-tory that started with the angels singing at Christ's birth. In Britain the carolers are called waits, because they return on December 26, Boxing Day, for their tips. By custom, they are pictured gathered around a lantern, but in many parts of Europe "star singers" take part in the job of caroling from house to house. They carry a great star in memory of the star of Bethlehem, and sometimes they even dress up as magi and other figures from the Nativity.

In Poland the cardboard star is made to revolve like a pinwheel, and usually one of the boy carolers wears a goat mask. A goat figure was originally the personification of the devil. This figure also appears in Sweden, where the rest of the caroling star boys dress in white and act out short biblical scenes as they sing. In Romania a wooden star is adorned with frills, little bells and a manger scene. In Finland the carolers, usually boys, raise large sums of money for charity with a play about the three kings.

In Mexico and South America, dance and drama surround the carolers. Throughout Scandinavia the old medieval meaning of carolers as ring dancers has translated into families gathering in a circle around the tree on Christmas Eve to sing traditional songs.

Today caroling too often has translated into attending large organized concerts rather than actually strolling about outdoors and singing in city streets and neighborhoods. That's too bad because the simplicity of caroling is one of the most inspiring and uplifting Christmas activities I know. That's what Phyllis Hobe discovered also.

A few years ago some neighbors invited me to go caroling with them a few nights before Christmas. I didn't think I should because I had so much to do, but the idea appealed to me. Somehow I found the time, and I'm glad I did. Because on that windy, bitterly cold night, as we trudged from house to house, singing those beautiful carols, greeted by smiles of surprised delight, I felt the joy of Christmas. For a few hours, I was free to think of nothing but the coming of Christ to earth and all that means.

Joy is the ability to give to others the love God gives to us, something I'd forgotten in the midst of holiday distractions and the usual complaint, "so much to do, and so little time."

But on this night the true meaning of Christmas returned to me—I saw that Christ isn't Someone we have to find. He has already found us. We don't have to follow a star or wait on a lonely hillside for a sign of His arrival. He is here, not only on earth, but in our hearts and in our lives.

But caroling isn't the only way that music makes the Christmas experience better. Music has a magic all its own any time of year. Particularly during the hectic holidays, music can truly be a blessing to our spirits and our bodies.

I grew up in a home where music was almost always playing. We listened to all kinds: jazz, rock 'n roll, instrumental, country, popular, show tunes; you name it, we heard it. As a result, I love music of all types. No matter what mood I'm in, a song can complement or lift my spirit.

Some recent research in Europe indicates that listening to music is not only good for the soul but also good for one's health, helping to regulate blood pressure and circulation. I find it most interesting that they found the best results are likely to come from people being able to listen to the music of their choice rather than music thought to be soothing. Now, what could be a simpler way to de-stress your holidays and put everyone in a better mood than popping in your family's favorite CDs and letting everyone sing along?

SIMPLICITY MADE SIMPLE

CAROLING IS A GREAT WAY to spread the true spirit of Christmas to your community while experiencing a bit of it yourself at the same time. One of my favorite

Christmas activities is having friends over and going caroling. First we have a cup of hot chocolate with freshly made whipped cream and a drop of peppermint syrup. Then we go caroling as a group.

GET INVOLVED IN YOUR CHURCH CHRISTMAS MUSICAL. That's what my husband Dave and I did for nearly seven years. He's got the voice and I have what some might call "the gift of bossiness." Every year our church put on a major Christmas musical, complete with a full orchestra. I directed, and Dave was one of the actor-singers. It was a wonderful way to get to know a hundred-plus people from church and partake of an opportunity to bring the Christ of Christmas to many others. Our friend David often wrote original music with particular singers in mind. It was a treat for them and a blessing to those who had the opportunity to hear these beautiful voices.

MAKE A DATE TO GO TO A CHRISTMAS CONCERT. Whether you prefer the classic Handel's *Messiah* or something jazzier—check your local newspaper for Christmas concerts and plan to attend with all your friends and family. One year nearly fifteen of us drove to Washington, D.C., for a performance. It was a wonderful experience and a memorable adventure.

DINNER GAME. For family dinner conversation, make a game of describing your current Christmas and your "dream" Christmas in terms of a song. "Joy to the World"? "I'll Be Home for Christmas"? "It'll Be a Blue Christmas without You"? "Deck the Halls"? . . .

WRITE A FAMILY CAROL. Choose some common tune you all know and write a Christmas carol that you can sing on Christmas Eve or Christmas morning. Who knows? Singing the masterpiece (or ditty) might become a family tradition.

WHISTLE WHILE YOU WORK. Turn on some carols as you wrap presents, bake cookies, decorate the tree, make crafts. Allow the Christmas spirit to pervade your home.

MAKE MUSIC A PART OF YOUR FAMILY GATHERING. Even though the instrument I played best was the accordion, I could never resist playing Christmas carols on a piano if one was available. My left hand had trouble keeping up with the right, but everyone sang along anyway. Now as our family has grown, there are a few far more talented pianists than I, and they willingly make music for us on Christmas Eve, so we can sing together as a family—in or out of tune, it doesn't matter.

Jesus, loving You puts music in our hearts.
Thank You for the carols that lighten our spirits.
Thank You for opportunities to sing Your praises
in the marketplaces and in our homes
through the holiday season while enjoying
the abundant life You have granted to us. Amen.

PART FOUR

A Sleighful of Toys: Gift Giving

GIFT GIVING AND CHRISTMAS. They have been intricately intertwined. That's one reason December can feel so, well, complicated. What will I give to whom? How much will I spend? When will I buy? The questions loom large. Stop. It is too easy to confuse a gift or its cost with the love and concern we really wish to express. Gifts don't always have to be something we buy. They can be something we make or even do for someone. Let's talk, then, about creating lists, checking them twice and making a budget of both time and money so that we can truly enjoy the art of giving to others.

The Gift of Giving

When they saw the star, they rejoiced exceedingly with great

joy. And they came into the house and saw the Child with

Mary His mother; and they fell down and worshiped Him;

and opening their treasures, they presented to Him gifts of

gold and frankincense and myrrh.

—MATTHEW 2:10–11 (NAS)

The ancient tradition of gift giving is filled with the desire to express our generosity, compassion and love to those we cherish. As we remember the simple birth of our Savior, we give thanks for the miracle of His life. And perhaps in a way our gift giving is a response to His great gift to all of us. There is hope in each gift given that it will also renew the miracle and the wonder of Christ's life and death and the impact it has had on our lives. Patricia Houck Sprinkle reflects on the meaning of God's gift:

What would it take for me to send one of my precious sons to a faraway land
to grow up among strangers, suffer their scorn and die from their hostility?

God gave a precious Gift out of an incredible love.
That's what Christmas is all about.

Thinking of what God gave can help me choose appropriate Christmas gifts for others. My choice is not between a book and a record or between a gift that's too extravagant and one that's cheap. My choice is between a gift that says, "Here's a present" and a carefully chosen one that says, "I love you."

You might say that the first Christmas gifts were those brought to Jesus by the wise men. The gifts the magi brought to the Christ Child were of royal quality. Frankincense was a fragrance important in establishing the proper atmosphere for worship; myrrh was a precious substance used for embalming; and gold continues to be unrivaled for its monetary significance. These gifts all had value and were a testament to the significance of this baby's divine mission.

It has been two millennia since the magi carried gifts to celebrate Christ's birth. But when we think about gift giving today, it's disappointing to see how we sometimes give out of habit rather than for the purpose of celebrating Christ's presence in our lives.

Nancy Loving Tubesing and Donald A. Tubesing, authors of *Kicking Your Holiday Stress Habits,* describe what they call the "Santa Claus trap." In terms of receiving gifts, we are like greedy children. "We are afraid we won't get what we want. We want everything and can't set priorities." In terms of giving gifts, "We try to please others with our gifts. We confuse the gift or the cost of the gift with the love and concern we really wish to give or receive."

Will Rogers once said, "The whole Christmas thing started in a fine spirit. It was to give happiness to the young, and another holiday to the old, so it was relished by practically everybody."

Who doesn't like to see the delight of a child opening packages?

Originally the children's gifts were inexpensive. As Marilyn Moore put it in a previous chapter, on the prairie even an orange was received with great joy. A handmade flannel nightgown or knitted mittens was a big deal. Now, for most of us, those basic necessities are taken for granted.

So where do we go from here? Let's start with examining why we should give gifts. In *The Complete Guide to Creative Gift Giving*, Cynthia Yates says, "We give to honor others, whether for personal accomplishment, life passage, or simply because of feelings of friendship and love. Our best gifts bear tidings of good will, of kindness, of praise, or respect. We give because we want to give." Just as the magi honored the Christ Child, so do we wish to honor those we love. That's why we often feel it's important to us to find exactly the right gift—we want it to be a reflection of our love and respect.

> Often our intentions are good, but we get caught up in a gift-giving frenzy.

But that is precisely what causes us to get caught up in a gift-buying frenzy. Our motivation and desires are good. Our timing, budget and planning are usually not. So when we find ourselves up against the clock, we run to the mall and buy something expensive, faddish, silly or inappropriate. The fact is that locating meaningful gifts takes time and planning—including financial planning. The good news is that there are some simple and effective ideas to help you avoid repeating these mistakes.

THE SECRET TO GIVING CHERISHED GIFTS

First, we need to recognize that not all gifts come with a price tag. Yates says in her book, "Kindness, compassion, unconditional love, and selfless sharing do not need big red bows or Christmas tree tinsel." Second, as the adage says, it's the thought that counts. We need to remember this as we contemplate the perfect gift.

One of my most cherished gifts is a simple red step stool that came from my hubby, Dave. It sits cheerfully in my kitchen waiting to be used, which is often, because I am very petite. I absolutely needed those extra steps. The color makes me happy, but it's the fact that Dave realized my dilemma and found a creative way to solve it that matters most, especially coming from a nearly six-foot-five-inch-tall man! His personal attention to my needs makes me feel loved.

This year my friend Jan was surprised with a gift from her mother: the family heirloom tablecloth that had been used every year at Christmas. This gift holds a lifetime of memories and will not only be cherished but will now become part of her family's tradition as well.

One year, when money was tight, Samantha McGarrity, found personal gifts in her own home, remembering how much she valued gifts her grandmother had given her.

> Thinking back to memorable gifts, I remembered how Grandmother, now ninety-five, always used to give me something that had belonged to her, something she had treasured and enjoyed through the years and then passed on to me to enjoy. Those gifts were the most prized!
>
> And so I looked about me, and discovered "gifts" among my possessions—a book of Longfellow's poems for Tim, a wind chime for Mother, cloisonné barrettes for Hillary, and so on down my list of family and friends. These gifts had been a part of my home for years, and all had given me some special joy. Now, giving them to people I loved helped me share that joy.
>
> I felt thankful for a grandmother who taught me how to truly give—with gifts from the heart.

SIMPLICITY MADE SIMPLE

JUST LIKE SANTA—MAKE A LIST! Many experts agree that the simplest way to be prepared for gift giving is to make a list of all the people (and events) over the next year for whom you will need a gift. Take into consideration possible weddings, anniversaries, engagements, holidays and birthdays, anything that might require a gift. Cynthia Yates suggests even including people to whom you will be giving no-cost gifts, like the older man down the street who would probably appreciate a gift of laughter and good conversation or good listening. Once the list is established, begin to brainstorm gift ideas and assign a possible cost for each. Study this list carefully. It will become your guide and tool for shopping.

CREATE A MONTHLY GIFT BUDGET. By simply adding a specific amount of money to your regular budget, you will resist the temptation to charge more than you can afford. It will also make it easier to pare down your gift giving where you can and keep focused on finding new and creative ways to give no-cost gifts.

KEEP AN EYE OUT FOR SALES and unexpected finds! With your gift list in hand, you can easily take advantage of after-Christmas sales and other seasonal sales throughout the year. Find a corner or a closet to stash your treasures until you need them. But it's very important to check this stash frequently to remind yourself of what you've got there. You might forget to give a prepurchased gift—as I did. My husband received last Christmas' gift of pajamas early this spring. They had been completely forgotten inside the gift closet! Now I mark my calendar after purchasing a gift for a certain person. This prevents impulsive buying for someone, when you've already bought a perfectly appropriate gift for him or her.

REFINE YOUR LIST. My extended family is large and continues to grow. We solved the overspending and overgifting problem by agreeing that only children under age twenty-one would receive gifts. Because each of my nieces and nephews has an uncle or an aunt as a godparent, we decided that on Christmas Eve the children would only receive one gift—from his or her godparent. We continued this tradition until they reached twenty-one, at which point they did not get a gift on Christmas Eve. Now that they are grown with children of their own, the tradition continues to the next generation. Remember that the holidays will quickly lose their luster when the material gift giving becomes the all-encompassing focus of the occasion.

DON'T LET GIFT-GIVING MYTHS TRIP YOU UP. You are not obligated to reciprocate just because someone gave you a gift. When this happens, simply accept the gift graciously. Another myth is thinking that there should be equality in gift giving. If someone gives you an expensive gift, you don't have to feel bad for giving something less expensive. Most likely, your friend and family already know your financial situation and wouldn't want you to spend more than you could comfortably afford.

Lord, forgive me for seasons past when I have given to others out of obligation rather than a cheerful heart. From this day forward, help me to focus on the value of those who receive my gifts rather than the expense of the gifts. Amen.

Gifts of Time and Talent

Rings and other jewels are not gifts,
but apologies for gifts.
The only gift is a portion of thyself.

—RALPH WALDO EMERSON

In an essay titled "Gifts," Emerson continues, "Therefore the poet brings his poem; the shepherd, his lamb; the farmer, corn; the miner, a gem; the sailor, coral and shells; the painter, his picture; the girl, a handkerchief of her own sewing. This is right and pleasing, for it restores society in so far to its primary basis, when a man's biography is conveyed in his gift, and every man's wealth is an index of his merit. But it is a cold, lifeless business when you go to the shops to buy me something, which does not represent your life and talent, but a goldsmith's."

By Emerson's standard the best possible and most appropriate gift might just be the gift of yourself or your talent. But how do you become a gift? The simplest answer is to give the gift of time. How many times have you said, "There just aren't enough hours in the day"? Even if you don't say it, you probably think it almost every day. The simple truth is that most people are chronically busy, which makes the gift of time a valuable commodity. Nancy Twigg, author of *Celebrate Simply*, says, "Many people would much rather give up some of their money than sacrifice a portion of their precious free time. Unlike store-bought presents, gifts of time are not duplicable." And for those who have more time than money, it's a simple way to show you care without overspending.

You may well know of the life story of Joni Eareckson Tada, who became a quadriplegic as a teen, as a result of a diving accident. She has written best-selling inspirational books and has started a ministry for people with disabilities. She's also an accomplished artist, painting with a brush that she maneuvers with her teeth. But you may not know how or why she started painting. It was the first Christmas season after her accident, and she was depressed that she wouldn't be able to shop and buy gifts. But realizing that Christ's Christmas gift had been Himself, she got to thinking about some way that she could "give herself." Her resources were limited, but the next day she put her heart into her physical therapy session—where instructors were urging her to paint a candy dish by manipulating the brush with her jaw. That initially feeble attempt blossomed into a gift that has blessed all of us who have seen her artwork.

GIVE WHAT NO ONE ELSE CAN

Some readers will admit that when it comes to Christmas gift giving, they have more time than money. If that is the case, simplifying your Christmas might well mean giving something you have made. When my friend Jan and her husband were just married and struggling financially, they took a lot of photos of their parents throughout the year. From the photos they made a decorative collage for every member of the family. Those gifts were among the most treasured for years. If you can draw, write, paint or craft, create a piece of art in honor of a loved one. Last year I knit an afghan for my mother-in-law for Christmas. It was supposed to be a surprise, but she surprised me instead when she dropped by for a visit. I wasn't home, and my husband didn't think anything of the fact that my knitting basket and the afghan-in-process were all laid out on the ottoman in the living room. My mother-in-law admired it and inquired about it. My husband let the cat out of the bag and told her it was for her! I was very disappointed, but she was thrilled. The moral of the story: It doesn't matter if someone knows in advance that you are making something special; in fact, that added anticipation may make the gift even better.

> Give what no one else can—the gift of yourself.

Another category of gifts does not involve making things but rather relies on the idea that our time and presence are in themselves gifts. When it comes right down to it, what some consider "free" gifts can be among the most expensive gifts to give because of the time commitment they involve. It might seem easier to buy and give a present. But the sense of gratification you receive from giving yourself and the smile of appreciation from the recipient are great rewards. Consider some of the ideas suggested by Kristin Tucker and Rebecca Lowe Warren, in *Celebrate the Wonder: A Family Christmas Treasury*: "There are hundreds of ways to become a gift. Enjoying a concert with a friend, teaching a neighbor to fish, babysitting for a relative."

If December hours are at a premium for you, you might give an IOU for a time later in the year. For under-the-tree presentation, you might create and wrap a well-appointed "promissory note" that describes the intent of your future commitment. The IOU might be for something that usually costs money such as babysitting, mowing grass, even grocery shopping. My friend Jan's grown sons surprised her this year by painting her bedroom for Christmas. It might involve a getaway adventure, maybe a summer picnic or a springtime afternoon at a local museum. Be creative.

A few years ago, while my grandmother Irene was still alive, I had the opportunity to travel for business twice a month to California to where she lived. I made sure to rent a car and stay a few days extra each time so I could visit with her. Those were some of the best and sweetest times of my life. Sometimes we sat and chatted or walked along the beach. Other times we went shopping—Grandma never owned or drove a car—so the opportunity to go far beyond the bus line was particularly exciting for her despite the fact that Grandma never spent much money. Just being together was a gift we gave each other. But the best part was when I would return home and unpack my suitcase. I always found a love note and a small token gift. Sometimes it was something that she loved and wanted me to have, and other times it would be something as simple as a small bottle of hand lotion. I cherished them all.

> Something as simple as a compliment, a telephone call or a word of encouragement will be appreciated for a long time thereafter.

The heart of the matter is to mix your creative juices with loving care to make a gift without measure. Something as simple as the gift of a compliment, a telephone call or a word of encouragement will be appreciated for a long time thereafter. For me, some of the best gifts are simply hearing from those far away. I have a friend I have known since kindergarten. She lives in Kemmerer, Wyoming. We haven't actually seen each other since our tenth high-school reunion; that was a lot of years ago. But we always touch base at Christmas. It's such a joy to catch up. Our hearts still remember a lifetime of experiences that we shared and we keep on sharing despite the distance of miles.

SIMPLICITY MADE SIMPLE

If you do give IOUs, make every effort to **KEEP YOUR COMMITMENTS**. Mark your calendar so you do not forget to make follow-up calls. It's up to you to initiate the scheduling of the get-together. "What would be a good time for you for us to make that museum trip?" If several scheduling calls result in no interest, you might write a note, and then leave the scheduling in the receiver's hands. You've made your offer clear, and you don't want to force your idea of a nice afternoon onto someone else.

Give a busy mom some peace and quiet. Perhaps you know someone who could use an afternoon alone. It might be your spouse, daughter or a parent. Give the person a coupon entitling him or her to two hours of peace and quiet while you take the kids for an afternoon. It doesn't even have to be a young person with children. Caretakers really appreciate and need an afternoon off. **A GIFT OF YOUR TIME** to take over for a few hours might just be a sanity saver. This, again, might be an IOU. One friend of mine, who is the primary caretaker for her ill husband, was thrilled when her three grown children gave her the gift of one weekend a month off while they care for their dad.

TACKLE A BIG JOB. Our small group is giving the gift of taking on a major project together at each other's homes. Coming up soon, a single-again mom will be getting her deck powerwashed and restained. Two weeks ago a new floor went into the family room of another small-group family with the help of the other guys.

GIVE MEANINGFUL GIFTS, suggest Nancy and Donald Tubesing: "Give presents (buy or make something) and give your presence (pledge your time and attention). Don't just give tickets to a cultural or sports event—plan to go along and share the experience together. Give the gift of words: affirmations, memories, thanks.

Give blood. Give groceries to the food pantry. Give a mother with toddlers an afternoon of childcare. Give new books to your school library. Give a hand to a neighbor in need." My mother always gave her young grandchildren the gift of an afternoon out with her. Sometimes it was to the ballet, other times the theater and sometimes it was a day of window shopping and lunch at the mall. I too enjoyed spending time with nieces and nephews, so we also gave each other the gift of time together. Each visit home included a "date" with one of them. They kept track of whose turn it was and planned the day.

For the family on Christmas morning, authors Tucker and Warren suggest wrapping a box with an **"OPEN ME FIRST"** tag attached. Place a few sheets of tissue and a note inside the box: "This box is filled with enough peace and love to last all year! Share it generously and you will find a renewed Christmas spirit this day!"

> Lord, You created the earth and all that is
> within it and gave it to humankind to enjoy.
> When there was nothing more for You to give,
> You gave Yourself. Help me to give to others
> as You have given so freely to me. Amen.

Christmas Shopping: In Line, Online, Out of Line?

He that handleth a matter wisely shall find good:

and whoso trusteth in the Lord, happy is he.

—PROVERBS 16:20 (KJV)

Perhaps no country has been as wrapped up in gift giving as Germany, a country known for its wonderful legends. In seventeenth-century Germany Christmas gifts, called Christ-bundles, included food, such as candy, sugarplums, cakes, apples and nuts, as well as dolls and other toys and clothing and shoes. And always tucked among the packages were educational items, such as ABC tables, paper, pencils and books. Ah, but attached to the bundle there was a Christ-rod, a twig that originally represented St. Nicholas, and that served as a pointed reminder for good behavior!

Boy, have we come a long way since then. Today we too often struggle to buy children the "perfect gift," because they already have everything imaginable. "Satisfying every want and desire of a child is unhealthy, but a very hoped-for gift that will cause a stir in a child's heart and smile on your face is a good thing," says Cynthia Yates, author of *The Complete Guide to Creative Gift Giving*. I agree. I still own the pair of roller skates that I desperately wanted when I was in fourth grade. For years I rented skates every Saturday morning at the rink. Receiving a brand-new pair of white and silver skates for Christmas that year was a dream come true. I used those skates up until eleven years ago. They certainly served me well. And although they still fit me, they are now obsolete because everyone is using inline skates, which I am completely inept at staying upright on. But just thinking about those roller skates makes me feel loved.

> If you find Christmas crowds overwhelming, consider catalog, TV or Internet shopping instead.

Shopping for the perfect gift can be one of the most tiring and frustrating experiences of the season. But there are ways to avoid the crowds, find more options and do it from the comfort of your own home. Consider catalog, television or Internet shopping instead of the mall.

When it comes to shopping by catalog, I'm an expert. I receive hundreds of mail-order catalogs every couple of months. The more I order, the more catalogs I receive. I am definitely on "the list." Did you know that there are nearly one thousand American catalogs? When I walk in the house, I often find myself thumbing through a catalog that's come in the mail before I even get my coat off, dog-earing pages, so I can easily find those tempting items later. Personally, I love shopping by mail.

Many experts thought that Internet sales would detract from catalog sales. Instead, many of us, including me, still prefer browsing through the print catalogs. It's simply not the same experience online. Pages take too long to load, and it isn't as clear or easy to see all the details. Having said that, if I cannot find what I am looking for in my paper catalog, I don't hesitate to go online to search. The convenience of online shopping is an added benefit for me.

But the catalogs are still my primary source of information and enjoyment. The whole catalog industry is far more sophisticated than ever before. This year's *Bloomingdale's* Christmas catalog included amazing quotations on "imagination," to inspire us to think more creatively about the way we dress. For example, one page, which pictured a willowy model standing on the rocks at water's edge, dressed in a black cashmere cropped cardigan with a white rib tank and black tailored pants, included a quote from Joseph Joubert: "Imagination is the eye of the soul."

I found it interesting that according to a survey by the Multi-Channel Merchant Consumer, only eight and a half percent of individuals who were polled describe the experience of catalog shopping as "less satisfying than shopping in a store." The majority of respondents, nearly sixty-two percent, describe catalog shopping as being on par with shopping in a store. I think it's simply because we don't have to get dressed and waste all that time driving around trying to find a parking space!

SHOPPING FROM THE COMFORT OF YOUR COUCH

Have you tried shopping from your television? You might be surprised at the experience. I know a lot about television shopping because I work at the biggest shopping network, QVC. They have been around for twenty years and reach more than eighty-seven million homes in the United States.

Many of our customer-viewers depend on us for shopping because they have health issues that make shopping in stores difficult or impossible. Many of our new customers find us as a result of an illness that kept them bedridden for a period of time. Television shopping is truly wonderful for these folks.

Television does have some advantages over other vehicles when it comes to shopping. Most important is its ability to educate, demonstrate and delineate the unique characteristics and benefits of the products. I love the fact that often the inventors or artists themselves go on air and present their products to the viewing audience. This gives buyers an opportunity to get to know and appreciate the people behind the product. I remember one gentleman who had been in the cleaning industry all his life. He brought his cleaning products to QVC and over time he has become so successful that he has hired someone else to do the television demonstrations. This enabled him to become a missionary, something he had dreamed of for years.

Online shopping, or e-commerce, also has advantages. Online shopping's biggest edge is the sheer number of products they can make available. Unlike bricks-and-mortar stores, they don't actually have to inventory or stock items. A good example of this is Amazon.com. A superstore bookstore usually carries about 175,000 titles. Amazon.com can carry three to five million different titles. Although some online stores do warehouse product themselves, many take the orders and have manufacturers ship directly to consumers.

SIMPLICITY MADE SIMPLE

VERIFY THE DELIVERY DATE. When you place an order, the vendor usually tells you when to expect delivery. Sellers are required to ship items as promised or within thirty days after the order date, if no specific date is stated. If the seller can't ship the goods within the promised time or the thirty-day deadline, the seller must notify you, give you a chance to cancel your order and provide a full refund if you choose to cancel. Most will do this via a postcard, which asks you to phone the retailer to confirm your decision to wait or to cancel. The seller also has the option of canceling your order and refunding your money. It's a good idea to allow for a couple of extra days in delivery time during December as even the best retailers can fall behind. Nothing can seem worse than giving someone an IOU because your gift is backordered.

FIND OUT WHAT YOU'VE BEEN MISSING. You can visit CyberCatalogs to compare and request more than seven hundred premier U.S. and international mail-order catalogs. Their link is www.cybercatalogs.com.

SHOP EARLY FOR THE HOLIDAY SEASON. Place your order early to make sure you get what you want. Check out a company's Web site for special Internet-only deals and to get additional information on catalog items. When you call a catalog's toll-free number to place your order, be sure to ask about any unadvertised deals or discounts. If you're ordering for Christmas delivery, place your order by December 19. And finally, keep the return information with the item just in case the recipient wants to make an exchange.

SHOP WITH COMPANIES YOU KNOW AND TRUST. Make sure that the company you buy from can provide the quality goods that you order.

CONSOLIDATE YOUR ORDER TO SAVE ON SHIPPING AND HANDLING. Order as many items as possible at one time from the same catalog. I use yellow sticky notes or simply dog-ear the pages as I browse the catalogs. When I am ready to order, it makes it easy to locate the items I have found interesting.

Shop wisely. **USE A SECURE BROWSER.** This is the software you use to navigate the Internet. Your browser should comply with industry security standards, such as Secure Sockets Layer (SSL). These standards scramble the purchase information you send over the Internet. Most computers come with a browser installed. Make sure that you're buying over a secure computer (server), and that you use a browser that supports 128-bit encryption, the strongest available today. Encryption translates your personal data, like credit card numbers, into something like a secret code as it is transmitted over the Web. If a Web site is using secure technology, its Web address begins with https and a tiny locked padlock appears at the bottom right of the computer screen.

KEEP YOUR PASSWORDS PRIVATE and avoid using a telephone number, birth date or a portion of your Social Security number. Pay by credit card, so your transaction is protected by the Fair Credit Billing Act. Keep a record. Be sure to print a copy of your purchase order and confirmation number for your records. You should also know that the Mail and Telephone Order Merchandise Rule covers online orders. This means that unless the company states otherwise, your merchandise must be delivered within thirty days; if there are delays, the company must notify you.

> Lord, sometimes I feel that the needs of others
> are so great that my small contribution is worthless.
> But deep inside of me remains the desire to give.
> Lord, I am grateful for the abundance of goods
> You have provided for us. Thank You for helping me
> to find fair prices and trustworthy merchants. Amen.

Rudolph's Gift

A gentle answer turns away wrath,

but a harsh word stirs up anger.

—PROVERBS 15:1

Most of us would agree with Solomon that it is better to respond to someone's anger with gentleness than with harshness. Despite the simplicity of this proverb, we all can become the victim or the cause of rude remarks during reindeer season. Think of Rudolph: He kept his spirit of Christmas despite the rudeness of his peers. Good manners should matter year-round. But during the holidays, we have an even greater expectation for the "spirit of Christmas" to invade our souls and make us gentle, patient and kind. However, the mere fact that we are attempting to fit in the joys of the season with the duties of parenting, shopping, decorating, entertaining, cooking and cleaning along with all our normal daily responsibilities sets us up for irritation.

A survey conducted by Public Agenda, called "Aggravating Circumstances: A Status Report on Rudeness in America, 2002," found that eight in ten people claim that lack of respect and courtesy is a serious problem. Six in ten say that in the past few years, strangers have become increasingly rude to one another. In fact, forty-one percent of people admitted to being rude themselves. Whether it is a minor slight by a salesclerk or a serious case of road rage, clearly many of us are intensely frustrated by the lack of respect we encounter, especially during the Christmas season.

> Often a salesclerk's attitude is directly related to the attitude of the customer in front of her.

The average retail store is prime territory for this uncivil attitude. Three-quarters of those surveyed said they had seen customers treat sales staff rudely. On the other hand, as many as sixty-four percent admitted to leaving a store because of the way sales staff had treated them. Part of the problem is that it's getting harder and harder for retailers to find good help during the holidays. I have found that it's best to shop in off-hours, like dinnertime, when the stores are less crowded. I've also found that the store clerks' attitudes and patience are directly related to my own.

While scrambling to locate a new outfit for the holidays, I went looking for a salesclerk to help me. The only one I could find was happily chatting on the phone. I waited patiently for about five minutes. Then, as kindly as I could, I interrupted her and inquired about where I might find a brown velvet jacket. Amazingly, she responded and pointed me in a direction where I found a few things to try on. When I realized I needed a key to get into the dressing room, I went back to the still-chatting salesperson. This time she simply handed me her keys!

The third time I approached her I was dressed in one of the pieces I'd found—asking for a desperately needed outside opinion. She finally hung up the phone and devoted herself to helping me for the next forty-five minutes. She cheerfully went from one department to the next, looking for a jacket that would be suitable for my size and age. Soon we were chatting and exchanging information. As she was ringing up my purchases, she handed me her card and said I should call her anytime I needed help.

This whole experience could have gone a very different way if I had adopted a pushy or sarcastic attitude or had rudely interrupted her, demanding attention. Instead, my smile and gentle approach showed respect and made the experience a good one for both of us.

In terms of Christmas gifts, I agree with Phyllis Hobe, who notes that Christmas means . . .

> . . . that we can give to one another, not things, exhaustion, short tempers or heroic achievements, but simply the kind of undemanding, tenderly caring love that God gives to us. This is the way each one of us can truly bring joy to the world.

THE GIFT OF GOOD MANNERS

It's true that it is often the other guy who is rude. But Sandra Morisset, a professional etiquette trainer in New York City, says, "It's all about self-awareness and treating others with respect. If you're not aware of your behavior, that's a problem." Most Americans rate their own manners as quite excellent, but studies indicate that rudeness is on the rise. Can we—ourselves—be part of the problem?

For most of us, the holidays involve traveling. Take it from me, as someone who travels a lot, I know that there is no time when travel is not stressful. It can be a nightmare during the holidays. Amy Ziff, editor-at-large for Travelocity, says, "It's important that we all take time to examine our own actions to see if there are things we can do to help modify or eliminate rude behavior on the road." The most festive and celebrated season of the year brings out some of the most not-so-merry behavior—especially among travelers.

Fortunately, there are a few remedies to help travelers. First, be sure to know the rules at airports regarding what can be included in carry-on bags ahead of time so you can move through security quickly and easily. Since sixty-five percent of people cited waiting in long lines and losing one's patience as the most common trigger for rude behavior, plan to arrive at the airport during an off-hour—even if it means being a few hours early for your flight. I often plan to arrive early at the airport and have a meal after checking in my baggage. I have found midmorning and midafternoon to be the most civilized times of day at the airport.

But why do we behave so badly? There are probably dozens of reasons. Cynthia Gorsso, founder of the Charleston School of Protocol and Etiquette in South Carolina, cautions against pointing the finger at any one person or cause. She says, "We all find people irritating; that's a fact. But the bottom line is, how you treat people is not about how they are, it's about how you are." And that takes us back to Proverbs 15:1: "A gentle answer turns away wrath, but a harsh word stirs up anger."

Caught in Christmas traffic one day Isabel Wolseley sensed her irritation rising until she noticed another woman's calm, which made her newly appreciate the gift of Christmas kindness:

> The traffic signal was a green dot in the distance, but the vehicles ahead of mine seemed rooted to the road. "What's the matter with you?" I muttered at their drivers. "You've got the light. *Go!*"
>
> Finally, the sluggish line did move, but half a block before I reached the intersection, the signal turned red. Lines of cars—four lanes deep and curb to curb—stretched to infinity in all directions. *This is like being in a herd of turtles. In fact*, I fumed, *at this rate, turtles could zip past me in a cloud of dust.*

Just then I noticed a harried young woman trying to exit a parking lot on my right. Four obviously tired youngsters chafed in car seats. The smallest of the quartet wailed while his siblings offered a Christmas cacophony of "Rudolph," "Jingle Bells" and "O Little Town of Bethlehem." *That mother has a worse problem than I do.*

When the light finally turned green, I caught her eye, then held my car in place and waved her in ahead of me. She flashed a radiant—and relieved—smile and popped into the opening I provided. Just before disappearing into the sea of cars, she blew me a kiss.

I actually enjoyed the rest of my trip home! Since then I've blown a few kisses to courteous drivers myself. It's such a simple way to "pass it on."

SIMPLICITY MADE SIMPLE

BE PATIENT. This is especially important when shopping. Everyone wants—and demands—attention, and the stores are almost always shorthanded. Always say "please" and "thank you." Avoid using your cell phone in public. If you must, go to a restroom or lounge area to guard against interrupting other customers. Even among cell phone users, many think that other people are using their cell phones discourteously.

BE A SAFE, COURTEOUS AND CALM DRIVER. Americans find rude and dangerous drivers to be number three on their list of uncivil actions—and holiday traffic is worse than any other time of the year. The simple way to avoid getting tangled in such a discourteous situation is not to offend other drivers. The Dane County Sheriff's Office in Madison, Wisconsin, offered these suggestions: Don't cut off others. When you merge, make sure you have plenty of room. Use your turn signal. If you make a mistake and accidentally cut off someone, try to apologize with an appropriate gesture. Don't drive slowly in the left lane. If you are in the left lane and someone wants to pass, move over and let the car go by. You may be "in the right," but you may also be putting yourself in danger by angering drivers behind you. It is not your job to keep them from speeding. Don't tailgate. Drivers get angry when you do this. Allow at least a two-car-length space between your car and the car ahead of you. Be cautious and courteous and only rarely use your horn. If another driver seems eager to get in front of you, say, "Be my guest." When you respond this way, after a while, "Be my guest" becomes your automatic remark and you won't be as offended by other drivers' rudeness. Give angry drivers a lot of room. If another driver tries to pick a fight, put as much distance as possible between your car and his. Do not, under any circumstances, pull off to the side of the road and try to "settle things." Get help. If you believe the other driver is following you or trying to start a fight, use your cell phone to call police or drive to a place where there are lots of people around. Then use your horn to get someone's attention.

GIVE KIDS A BREAK. Accept the fact that most children simply act their age. The problem is that we expect them to act like little adults when the reality is that they cannot. Christmas is just another day for children less than a year old. Toddlers, although lovable and cute, are curious. They are also demanding and exasperating. The best advice in anticipation of a young Christmas visitor is to childproof your home and don't try to make too much of Christmas until next year. Two-year-olds will be very excited about everything, but they care more about what glitters and shines than what awaits them inside boxes. It is also typical that two-year-olds don't share well. They are normally stubborn and don't necessarily like to shop. Three-year-olds want to be involved. Let them help decorate and wrap packages. Four-year-olds are simply silly, eager and fun. They love the holidays. The only problem is that they have more energy than any three adults. So be prepared to eat your Wheaties or granola. Five-year-olds will actually enjoy sitting on Santa's lap and will also be happy to help keep Grandma's gift a secret. They love secrets!

BE A GOOD GUEST. Always RSVP, arrive on time, and call if you are going to be late. Don't bring a surprise guest! Bring a giving attitude and your good cheer will contribute to the joy of the season. If you have been invited to be a houseguest, be sure to take along an appropriate gift. Offer to do chores such as washing dishes, while keeping your room and bathroom tidy. Keep children from being too noisy or disruptive. If you are hosting the party, be sure to find out in advance if anyone has special dietary needs. At family gatherings, avoid topics that you know will set off someone. Do not boast about your big raise or talk about how badly you are doing financially. Don't bad-mouth any family members who are not present or embarrass family members who are. And no matter how tempting, do not go on and on about how amazing your children's or grandchildren's talents or accomplishments are.

> Lord, I realize that I could be viewed as rude
> even when I'm not aware of it but too often
> I simply lose control and offend others. Please forgive me
> for this selfish approach to holidays, and keep me
> from putting my own desires first. I pray to forgive
> others as You have forgiven me. Amen.

All Wrapped Up

The manner of giving is worth more than the gift.

—PIERRE CORNEILLE (1606–1684)

If you don't think presentation matters, think again. "Psychologists, writers and seminar leaders all caution that we have only seven to seventeen seconds of interacting with strangers before they form an opinion of you," says David Saxby, president of Measure-X, a company that specializes in customer service and sales. "Worse yet, it takes them three times as long to change their minds about you." Image may not be everything—but it is important. Showing up for a new job interview wearing a wrinkled, unwashed pair of pants with an unmatched blouse is something you would never do. Yet many of us have given or received a gift that wasn't dressed for presentation. You wouldn't want to disappoint the recipient before they even see the gift, would you?

When I think about all the gifts God has given us, there is no doubt that they have been painstakingly wrapped: the sky, the plants, the animals, the mountains and the seas are all breathtakingly beautiful in every detail. When it comes to giving a gift, the manner in which we present it can add or detract from the gift—no matter how great or modest it is. Someone once told me that if we aren't up to the challenge, at least let's look like we are. That challenge works for gifts as well. The simplest and least expensive gift can leave the best impression if it is presented in a way that shows thoughtfulness and effort.

Some may ask, "Why wrap at all?" For starters, most of us like to unwrap. Who doesn't like to discover *hidden* treasure? Most children, and even adults, like the intrigue of those Russian dolls, one inside another. Of course we know that the smaller one is just a cut-down version of the larger, but there's a delight in the unveiling.

One of my assistant Patty's favorite memories of gift giving at Christmas is the way her grandparents wrapped gifts for her mother and her mom's two sisters. The three daughters loved to guess what was in a package before they opened it and were often correct in their guesses (maybe because Patty's family always exchanged lists and pretty much gave gifts right from the lists).

Patty's grandparents felt that this took the fun out of opening the gifts. Thus began the tradition of each of the daughters receiving one special "creatively" wrapped gift from their parents each year. Cousins, grandchildren and husbands looked on as Patty's mother and her sisters opened gigantic, beautifully wrapped boxes, only to find another beautifully wrapped package inside of that and so on, until finally they reached the gift. One year, Patty's grandparents actually encased the gifts in plaster-of-paris and provided a small pick axe for each of their daughters to chip away until they got to the present! No one even remembers what the presents were anymore, but they all love reminiscing about how much fun it was to watch the elaborate process of unwrapping the gifts. So ultimately the gift wrap became part of the gift, adding anticipation and excitement to the holiday celebration as well as many cherished memories for the entire family.

THE MANNER OF GIVING

You may say, "All well and good, but let's get practical." Okay, if we're simply practical, packaging can be important because it protects our precious cargo. And ribbons—they're pretty, yes, but before the days of easily accessible tape, ribbon and string served the very functional purpose of keeping the package from falling open.

Most people will find this rather amusing but, despite the fact that I am an interior designer, I am not the world's best gift wrapper. Part of the problem is simply that I usually don't have the time to dedicate to the process. I put my heart into choosing the gifts and pray that the gift is good enough to take the attention away from the wrapping.

That said, I do enjoy making unique and fun name tags. Since Dave and I have been married, I always write a little poem that gives clues as to what his gift might be, making him guess before he opens it. He loves this little game and looks forward to it every year. Last year I discovered the "art" of name-tag making on my computer. It started with my typing the little poem in red or green ink and then cutting it into a holiday shape. This year I found holiday templates and decorations that I could add to the tags. Dave was completely amazed and couldn't figure out how I could make something so creative!

For my great nieces and nephews, I reused old Christmas gift bags and then personalized each one with a big decorative tag with their names emblazoned on them. They were so cute and simple to make. I love gift bags! Simply add a ribbon or a bow and you have the perfect package.

I sometimes purposely set aside a day for wrapping to better enjoy the process.

> You can personalize packages with items that suit your style: leaves or berries, pinecones, even seashells.

For my friend Jan, I found an old box from cosmetics, with gold and black stripes. The lid of the box had the name of the cosmetic company on it, so I wrapped the lid with gold foil. Then I used an old bow, made from gold-wired ribbon, to complete it. It was beautiful and so easy to do. In fact, I managed to wrap all the presents and send Christmas cards this year without buying anything new, no new wrapping paper and no new cards. (I used up all the leftover cards and paper from previous years.)

My assistant Patty is an expert at wrapping. She says the trick is to use lots of tape. Believe me, opening one of her packages is like breaking out of jail. I usually just give up and tear at it rather than trying to open it nicely. Because she is so good and efficient at wrapping, my husband has found that the way to simplify his wrapping is to give it to Patty for her to wrap!

I will admit, I do love a pretty package. And it really is not hard or complicated to accomplish the art of package decoration. Simply follow your own style. If you love the outdoors, then take a walk and gather natural items to use as package adornments. Leaves, twigs, berries, acorns and pinecones are just a few of the additions that make a package special. As I've said, I love the beach and always have a large collection of shells at hand. By gluing a few shells onto a lovely ribbon, I can create a unique package that reflects my style.

SIMPLICITY MADE SIMPLE

You may find it relaxing and energizing to **CREATE YOUR OWN WRAPPING PAPER.** It's as simple as grade-school art. There are so many wonderful patterns and designs of rubber stamps to use. Choose vivid paint colors and apply to plain white craft paper or butcher's paper for a crisp and clean look. Keep it simple with only one or two colors or, if you feel confident, mix it up! I also like reverse printing. Dip your pattern stamp into a dish of bleach. Then print on colored tissue or other colored paper. The bleach will remove color where you stamp, creating a unique effect. Brown package wrapping paper also works well for creating your own style.

If youngsters need a project to keep them occupied for a few hours, give them some large sheets of paper and **SET UP THE CHILDREN WITH CRAYONS OR PAINTS** to make wrapping paper for their own gifts and even for yours. Grandma will love it. Or young children might get a kick out of wrapping their own presents in the Sunday newspaper comics.

MORE PAPER IDEAS include: newsprint paired with red ribbon or attractive magazine pages, which are great for small items, as well as maps, pictures or pages from decorative calendars. One of my favorite wrappings is leftover wallpaper. As an interior designer I have an endless supply. But you can find remnants at your local paint and wallpaper store. It's sturdy and different from standard wrapping paper, even though you use it the same way. In particular, I love to wrap boxes in it. I purchase inexpensive lidded boxes and then dress them up with coordinating wallpapers. The paper makes the boxes sturdier. Then to the top of the lid, I add ribbons, flowers, tassels, bells, greenery—any sort of decorative detail that I happen to have. Many people have actually thought the gift was the box itself, and I had to encourage them to look inside!

USE UNUSUAL CONTAINERS. I read about one woman who used the roll from leftover wrapping paper as a gift container for her teenage daughter's socks! She pinned together several pairs of socks and stuffed them in the roll. Imagine the fun her daughter had as she pulled and pulled one pair after the other from the tube. Containers are a great way to keep people guessing as to what the gift is. I also love using a container as the wrapping. For example, a pillowcase is perfect for so many kinds of gifts. Be sure to include the matching pillowcase as well, as an extra gift. Kitchen towels are fun and festive and make great wraps and bag stuffers.

BOX IT UP! I love hatboxes. They're not only beautiful and hold a lot of gifts, but they also are great organizers for the receiver to use later. I am always on the lookout for pretty boxes. I find them at craft stores, box stores, even at some of the deep discount or dollar stores.

SOFTEN IT UP AND BUTTON UP! Fabric is another beautiful way to wrap up things. You can upholster it to a box simply by padding the box with quilt batting first. I use a spray adhesive to keep the batting in place and then wrap the fabric around and glue the edges to the inside of the box. If you sew, you probably have an abundance of fabric pieces to choose from. If not, your local fabric store always has bins and bins of inexpensive remnants available. A scarf or bandanna is another great way to wrap a gift in a gift. I also collect buttons—who doesn't?—and every time I purchase a piece of clothing I get an extra button. Anyway, they are so much fun to use as a decorative item on packages. Anchor your bows with buttons, spell out the word JOY with buttons—however you use them, they are simply fun!

BAG IT! Bags have really gained in popularity, and as a result the prices just keep going up. Why not buy inexpensive, unadorned bags and decorate them yourself? Or look for bargains throughout the year. Recently a friend told me she purchased a fifty-nine-piece all-occasion gift bag collection with matching tissue paper for $26.13. That averaged out to fifty-seven cents a bag!

Lord, the greatest gifts may be simply wrapped,
as You were wrapped in swaddling clothes.
And the simplest of gifts may be wrapped extravagantly,
as the free gift of salvation is wrapped in the sacrifice
of Your life. I pray that all who receive my gifts
will see them as Christ-bundles of Your love. Amen.

Children and Gift Giving

". . . remembering the words the Lord Jesus himself said:

'It is more blessed to give than to receive.'"

—ACTS 20:35

God's gifts of forgiveness, love and new life come to us regardless of who we are and what we have done. If we believe that our gifts represent what God has given us, then we must, above all, hope to teach our children the importance of giving in a season that, for many children, revolves around receiving. Where does Santa fit into the picture? Does it mean that we must destroy children's fantasies about the cheery red-suited man? Not in my opinion.

Kristin Tucker and Rebecca Lowe Warren, authors of *Celebrate the Wonder*, feel that "Santa can be a child's key to seeing the giving side of gift exchanges. As our example of a giver, he demonstrates the 'love and generosity and devotion' that parents try to instill in their children."

Children are smarter than we often give them credit for. They can discern a great deal about the practicalities of gift giving while still believing in Santa.

The key is in how we approach the inclusion of Santa Claus in our holiday traditions.

CHILDREN LOVE THE JOY OF GIVING

Our Santa Claus (a Dutch-language version of St. Nicholas) is a modern characterization of a fourth-century bishop of the Christian church in Myra, a land of "green hills, warm sun and soft sea breezes" in what is now the country of Turkey. In *A Gift from St. Nicholas*, Cristine Bolley says that "St. Nicholas understood that life's real treasure is found in doing what is right in the eyes of God, and he discovered that joyful peace comes from loving others. He is remembered fondly for his anonymous efforts to give away his inherited wealth."

In the Christian liturgical calendar that marks saints' feast days, St. Nicholas Day is observed on December 6. On St. Nicholas Eve, the Dutch traditionally put out their shoes, which were filled with goodies the next morning, much as our children's stockings are brimming on Christmas. Nowadays, to help their children to place their visions of Santa in a Christian framework, some families and churches make St. Nicholas Day a part of their Christmas preparations. As a December 6 tradition, they read or tell the story of the bishop's generous gift giving in the name of Jesus.

If children's images of Santa are focused on his generosity, the wonder of being remembered, the mysteries of his work and the surprises he brings, they will better understand that Santa doesn't bring *everything* they want—nor should he. Indeed, if we teach our children to be *Santa's helpers* and aid him in making Christmas special for those less fortunate, they will learn the art of giving as well.

Many years ago, when my goddaughter was about six, her parents divorced. It was Alexa's first Christmas with just her mother, and she was becoming a bit skeptical about the whole Santa thing. She wanted desperately to get her mother a pair of pretty earrings for Christmas but didn't have the resources. I suggested she pray and ask God to let Santa know her desire. Though a bit doubtful, she prayed. On Christmas afternoon as we were exchanging gifts at my house, Alexa found a package under the tree with a tag that said, "To: Mom, From: Santa and Alexa." Alexa's eyes were wide with amazement as her mother opened the gift—a beautiful pair of dangling earrings! Wonder, mystery and blessing were all wrapped up in that pair of earrings. Alexa's faith in God and Santa were sealed for at least another year. In ways she didn't even understand, she had been Santa's helper.

Someday, when your children are grown, you might be surprised at what they remember about their childhood Christmases. Marjorie Holmes was. One year, her children and grandchildren gathered inside and someone pulled out old home movies newly transferred to videotape. She explained what happened next:

> Laughing and pointing, we sat reliving the merry commotion: hanging up stockings; trimming the tree; rescuing the cat from its tangle of tinsel; church pageants and plays; little angels singing; bathrobed shepherds waving as they marched onstage; Mickie dancing in *The Nutcracker Suite*.
>
> Then, when the show was over, they all began to discuss other Christmases. "Remember the years we adopted some poor family? How everybody got busy making or buying presents? You and Daddy let us pick out the turkey, and we were so proud, but one time Mallory dropped it in the mud. Sure wish we had a shot of that!"
>
> "Me too," his sister spoke up. "But what I remember most are those Raggedy Anns and Andys we made. I helped Mother sew them, you younger kids did the stuffing and she took you along to deliver them. Boy, were you excited!"

"I was selfish," Melanie confessed. "I wanted to keep my Andy. But I was never so thrilled as when I handed him over!"

On and on they went, recalling things I'd almost forgotten. And listening, I suddenly noticed: Not once did they mention anything they got. Not even a first bicycle or special doll. Instead, to my surprise, the memories they treasured most were the fun they had in giving.

"Oh, Mother," Melanie was laughing, "doing things like that was the best part of Christmas."

"It sure was," the others agreed, expressing only one regret: How nice it would be now to see movies of those times too.

Then several of them expressed it: Yes, but we didn't need them. We were doing something more important. The pictures were already engraved on our hearts.

It doesn't get any better than that—children who have the gift of giving etched on their hearts. We all pray that our children will never know need, but we certainly want them to be aware of it. The seductions of status may entice, but soon diminish. It is only God's abiding love in our hearts that breeds the greatest extravagance of all—charity.

SIMPLICITY MADE SIMPLE

HELP YOUR CHILDREN MAKE A LIST of people to give to this Christmas. Besides including close family and friends, neighbors and teachers, be sure to list a charity or needy family as well. Together, take the time to talk about each person on the list and remember times you shared with them. This helps make the people more relevant to your children's lives and will also help inspire gift ideas for each.

HELP YOUR CHILDREN "PLAY SANTA" by giving gifts in secret. This is a perfect way to teach the gift of giving by placing the focus on the giving and not on the giver. Family members and friends will enjoy such a gift. But it's also a great way to give to a neighbor or needy family without making someone feel obliged in any way or uncomfortable.

GUIDE YOUR CHILDREN'S GIFT CHOICES. Explain that a gift should express your care and desire to make Christmas special. Personalized greetings mean a lot and don't have to cost a lot. For example, if you're handy with a computer, creating a DVD collage of pictures or a collection of music is a great way to get a child's creative juices flowing. Both my brother and my sister have made music CDs for me. I cherish them and enjoy listening to them. Although they each chose completely different music, each collection is perfect for me! Grandparents and aunts and uncles especially appreciate artwork by the children. Because I don't have children of my own, receiving a handmade gift from a child is always a special treat for me.

For years, my friend Jan and several other Santa's Helpers gathered together with their young children to make Christmas gifts for all their friends and family. I was always amazed at what they produced. One year I received a "partridge in a pear tree." It was cut out of wood and assembled with little partridge birds glued to several of the branches. The dads cut the parts and the children painted them and then the moms helped the children assemble them. Even the packaging was special. They placed the trees inside brown paper bags for which they had rolled the tops down, to give them a stronger edge. From green crinkled tissue paper they formed large strands of ribbon, which they strung through a hole on either side of the top of the bag. Then they tied it with a raffia bow.

TEENS MIGHT OFFER TO GIVE THE GIFT OF LABOR. There are so many ways to give this gift. Offer to help a neighbor clean up a yard, rake leaves, shovel snow or even decorate the house for Christmas. Caring for pets or plants during holiday travels can mean a lot. Babysitting, grocery shopping and cleaning windows are all excellent, thoughtful gifts.

HELP CHILDREN SHOP. Children love giving something they have picked out themselves. Many churches and schools arrange a Santa store where children can shop. If you don't have the store in your area—consider starting one. Our local Christian school organized a group of volunteers that craft, buy and plan for the children's shop all year long. Then in early December the store is open for an entire week. And it's not just for children—anyone can shop there. My friend Jan's beautiful handmade wooden Christmas partridge and pear tree creations were part of one year's selections. It is simple but elegant, and it fits perfectly on my kitchen windowsill every year. Another year, I received a beautiful little clay-potted candle that was painted a pretty shade of blue with silver wash and a white bow, which sits on the corner of my desk. Other ideas that help to stretch a child's budget: import stores such as Ten Thousand Villages (a missionary fund-raising project of the Mennonite Church, www.tenthousandvillages.com), magazine counters, candle stores, road maps, seeds, cookie cutters, spiced teas, measuring tapes or even a bowl of seashells.

To **FOCUS CHILDREN ON THE REAL MEANING OF CHRISTMAS**—giving rather than receiving—set aside a few moments before opening presents to reflect on the Christmas story of God's gift to us. Say a prayer as you gather around the tree. Read the Christmas story from a family Bible. Sing carols on the porch or simply pause to be thankful for Christ's birth.

EVALUATE YOUR OWN GIFT GIVING. Nothing teaches as much as what we do. If we tell our children that gifts don't have to be expensive to be thoughtful, but then they hear us comment that we "haven't spent enough," they will learn that gifts must be expensive. Make sure your actions match your personal values. Start by shortening your own list of "I wants." Then plan to make a contribution to a charity or someone less fortunate than yourself. Purchase only gifts that are made or sold to help others, such as those bought through nonprofit organizations. Give the gift of your time to a hospital or nursing home. This can be a family or even a neighborhood effort. If you're having a party, ask each guest to bring something that can be placed in a gift basket for the homebound, hospital patients or even prison inmates. You could also hold a garage sale or craft bazaar to raise money for world hunger, cancer patients or your favorite charitable organization.

> Lord, I want to give good gifts to my children.
> Even more than that, I want them to learn to be
> generous, to know that it is more blessed to give
> than to receive. Help me to teach them those lessons
> by my words and also by my example, in the way
> I celebrate a simple Christmas. Amen.

Don't Forget Yourself

This season is all about gifts. Gifts that nurture the souls of
both the giver and given. Perfect gifts. The gifts of Spirit.

—SARAH BAN BREATHNACH

In this final section of the book we've talked a lot about gift giving, and I want to wrap up the subject with some simple ideas for what you can give yourself for Christmas. In previous chapters we've touched on some but not all of these self-care concepts, attitudes and activities that nurture the soul of you—the person who feels some responsibility for "making" Christmas for others. What can you give yourself for Christmas?

For starters, how about giving yourself a gift that involves learning how to receive graciously. Think about how many times you have found yourself saying, "No thank you, I can do this myself," when someone offered to help you.

Just recently, I offered to do the dishes after having a home-cooked meal with an older couple who have trouble getting around. Despite her physical struggle, the lady of the house just could not allow me to do the dishes. Why? I don't know for sure, but I suspect that part of the reason is that she simply has her own way of doing things. Yesterday, my goddaughter Lex was telling me about how she helped a friend fold laundry this past week. Much to Lex's surprise, her friend refolded everything that she had helped her with. Lex said, "I don't know how her soon-to-be-husband is going to handle her need to have everything perfect!"

I think learning to be a good receiver meets Sarah Ban Breathnach's standard of a gift that could nurture both you and someone else. In her Web site newsletter, Cheryl Richardson, the author of *Life Makeovers*, personal coach and lecturer, says, "One of the greatest gifts we give to others is our willingness to let them give to us." She suggests that we need to learn to stop, take a deep breath and try something new like: "Yes, I'd love help with the dishes," and, "Thank you for offering to make life easier."

If you're overwhelmed with Christmas preparations, try being humble enough to accept someone's offer of assistance.

FILL YOUR HOLIDAYS WITH SERENITY

Learning to master the art of laziness during the Christmas holidays may indeed be another gift to give yourself. For example, why not give yourself permission to sleep an hour or two longer than you normally would? Or if you still struggle with letting others help you clean up after dinner, try letting the dishes sit on the table long after the holiday meal is over, so you can enjoy talking with your guests rather than slaving in the kitchen. If you start cleaning up alone, you make your guests feel uncomfortable or worse. Soon they will feel so guilty that they will be compelled to clean with you instead of visiting with you. The whole point of inviting people to your home is to enjoy them! Of course if they cheerfully volunteer to help you, then make the best of both ideas and receive the offer for help gracefully, and combine the work in the kitchen with holiday stories or something that you all enjoy talking about.

Another gift: Be selective with the activities that you have been invited to and choose only to attend those that you know will be a wonderful experience. My sister Lorie is very good at taking care of herself during the holidays by not allowing herself to become overwhelmed with too many parties. She knows that parties stress her out, so she is careful about which invitations she accepts. She never hesitates to say that it would simply be too much for her. She knows her limitations and honors them. I give her a lot of credit for this. Protecting herself keeps her more relaxed. The more relaxed she is, the more loving her attitude is toward others. She prefers to be able to give the kinder, more loving part of herself to those she loves.

> Make self-care a priority during the holidays, or you may find yourself easily overwhelmed.

In December some of our self-care activities can be lost in all the hustle and bustle of holiday preparation. Yet taking the best care of ourselves during the Christmas season can contribute greatly to counteracting the sensation of being overwhelmed. Amidst all the preparations, shopping, wrapping and celebrating, why not give the gift of pampering? Sharing this gift with your mother, sister or best friend by arranging for a massage, pedicure or simply a day at the movies can easily nurture both of you.

And some of the best "mutual gifts" don't have to cost money. Try trading a massage or pedicure with each other. It's a simple and effective way of helping your body relax while investing in quality time together. In our fast-paced world, especially around the holidays, we drag our bodies around nonstop to the point of near exhaustion. To keep our energy up, we must practice extreme self-care.

As I urged in the beginning of this book, define clearly for yourself what seasonal experiences are important to you. If you don't know what you really want during the holidays, then it will be much harder to determine which invitations are or are not in alignment with your desires. By clearly pinpointing your preferences in writing, you'll have a place to start your evaluation. Remember also to share your desired holiday preferences with your spouse and other loved ones, asking them what their desires are too.

The secret to a happy holiday is learning to collaborate and to create a plan that is uniquely yours with a goal to experience more serenity, more joy and more opportunities to nurture the souls of those you love. But, most important, it is to remember the greatest gift ever given, the gift of the Christ Child born in a manger. Take time to simply sit and ponder this amazing miracle. I pray that you will find an opportunity for silence to quiet your mind, your heart and your spirit long enough to reconnect with the reason we celebrate and to sing His praises along with the angels.

SIMPLICITY MADE SIMPLE

Make yourself a promise to **TAKE ENOUGH QUALITY TIME FOR YOURSELF.** You deserve time away—alone. This is not being selfish; it is simply a way to commune with yourself and God. If you don't take time to go to the well for water, you will not have what is essential to quench the thirst of your soul. A dry soul has no resource for nurturing others. Throughout December, consider spending a little time each day contemplating a few verses of the Christmas story, as found in Matthew or Luke or in Old Testament prophesies such as those found in the words of Handel's *Messiah*.

Recognize that **YOU ARE NOT SUPERHUMAN.** You cannot provide unlimited care for everyone. You have limits. Acknowledging those limits helps to reduce anxiety and improve the love you give. Be proactive in taking steps to lessen your stress.

Don't be embarrassed or ashamed to ASK FOR HELP. Remember this is an opportunity to practice the act of generosity received by letting others give the gift of helping. Be willing to share the care.

KEEP YOUR NUTRITION GOALS ON TRACK. Many things can make this challenging: extra social events, tempting treats or travel. The holidays in general interfere with our regular eating habits. Don't skip meals, especially breakfast. If you do, you will only be hungrier later and more likely to overindulge in unhealthy foods. Pace yourself when faced with tempting goodies and sweets. Seek out healthier food choices such as the fruit or veggie trays. To boost your much-needed energy, be sure to increase your carbs and protein. Practice paying attention to when your body is hungry or comfortably full and respond accordingly. Try to put less focus on the food and more on enjoying conversation and other activities.

Choose how to **SPEND YOUR TIME WISELY**. Build time into your schedule to relax and enjoy the festive season. Give yourself the gift of extra time with loved ones who make you feel great. Stay in touch with a friend who's easily accessible for venting. My friend Jan and I have a mutual pact that whenever one of us needs to vent, we make ourselves available. Sometimes it's just a few emergency minutes in the driveway for debriefing our anxiety. You might even consider scheduling time for just such an occasion.

DO WHAT MAKES YOU SMILE. If running outside to make snow angels with your children or grandchildren is something you love to do, then do it. If taking a long hot bath in the middle of the day with your favorite bath scent, candles and music makes you feel good, do it. Take time for yourself each day to slow down and calm your body, mind and spirit. You will need this time more than ever during the holidays to maintain a healthy lifestyle—and frame of mind. Worship with family and friends. This will lift you above the countless holiday details and allow you to focus on God and others. Celebrate the things that are truly important—family, friends, giving and, most of all, love. Do something for your health, something for your heart and something for your soul. I promise that your holiday stress will drop and your joy will increase abundantly.

Lord, I will give wisely this holiday,
looking for ways to nurture the ones that I love
with gifts that strengthen them. I will also look
for ways to set good examples for those in my realm
of influence so they see that Your goodness and
mercy keep me in perfect peace. Amen.

Conclusion

Joy to the world. Silent night. Angels we have heard on high . . . Gloria. Let us adore him. Let us rejoice. Chestnuts roasting. Jingle bells. Deck the halls. Packages tied up with strings. Home for Christmas. Merry Christmas! We want it all—and every year. But having it all makes us feel exhausted, not exhilarated.

If you've learned just one thing from this book, I hope it is that you can have the best Christmas ever even if it's not the perfect Christmas or the most elaborate one.

The good news is that we have been given the perfect gift for making the best Christmas ever—Christ. As we remember the simple birth of the Savior, we can give thanks for the miracle of His life. But we can also offer hope with each gift we give for a renewal of His Spirit in the lives of those we love. Simply remind them of the blessing of the miracle, the hope and the wonder of Christ's life and death, and the impact it has had on our lives.

So rather than letting the sheer number of demands made on you during the holiday season hamper your spirit, find the joy that is hidden deep in your heart and share it with all those around you. Worship Christ, renew old friendships, revive or start new personal and family traditions, create a festive mood, give gifts with joy, receive them with gratitude and let the light of Bethlehem shine over you and all of your celebrations this year.

Bibliography

Bence, Evelyn, *Leaving Home*, (Carol Stream, Illinois: Tyndale House Publishers, 1986).

Betters, Sharon, *Treasures in Darkness*, (Phillipsburg, New Jersey: P & R Publishing, 2005).

Bolley, Cristine, *A Gift from St. Nicholas* (Colorado Springs: Honor Books, 2001).

Brown, Handel H., *A Recipe for a Merry Christmas* (Grand Rapids: William B. Eerdmans Publishing, 1960).

"Can You Learn to Be Creative?" www.closertotruth.com.

"Celebrating the Holidays in an Interfaith Family," www.babycenter.com.

"Children and Depression During the Holidays," www.medicalmoment.org.

"Coping with Depression and the Holidays," www.aagponline.org.

"Depression and the Holidays," www.medicalmoment.org.

Fiese, Barbarba H., Thomas J. Tomcho, Michael Douglas, Kimberly Josephes, Scott Poltrock and Tim Baker, "A Review of 50 Years of Research on Naturally Occurring Family Routines and Rituals: Cause for Celebration?" *Journal of Family Psychology*, (2002): Volume 16, No. 4.

Hammon, Christopher, "Handling Holiday Stress," www.oates.org.

"Hang 'em High (and Low)" *Real Simple Magazine,* December (2004).

Hawxhurst, Joan C., *The Interfaith Family Guidebook* (Kalamazoo: Dovetail Publishing, 1998).

"Heart Health: Music Is Good for Your Heart," www.healthierlife.co.uk.

Heller, David, *Talking to Your Child about God: A Book of Families of All Faiths* (New York: Bantam, 1988).

Kaufman, Taube S., *The Combined Family* (New York: Insight Books, 1993) .

Lancaster New Era, Monday March 7, (2005): A4.

"Make a Strong First Impression with Customers," public-utilities.press-world.com.

Orman, MD, Morton C., "A Special Report: How to Keep Stress and Tension from Ruining Your Holiday Season," www.stresscure.com.

Papernow, Patricia, "Doing the Stepfamily Holiday Shuffle or…Two Homes for the Holidays," Stepping Stones Counseling Center, www.stepfamilies.com.

"Poll Reveals Rudeness Causes and Effects," www.couplescompany.com.

Richardson, Cheryl, *Life Makeovers* (New York: Broadway Books, 2002).

"Rein in Rudeness—Start with the Holidays," www.wcpn.org, (2004).

"Road Rage," www.danesheriff.com.

Robinson, Jo, and Jean Coppock Staeheli, *Unplug The Christmas Machine* (New York: William Morrow and Company, Inc., 1991).

Rosenbaum, Mary Helene, and Stanley Ned Rosenbaum, *Celebrating Our Differences: Living Two Faiths in One Marriage* (New York: Ragged Edge Press, 1998).

"Rudeness on the Rise," www.forbes.com, (2003).

Stoppler, MD, Melissa C., "The Season to Be Tired," www.stressabout.com.

Thouin, Juanita "Holiday traditions: more important than you think" [Quote by Anna Stewart, *Inspired Parenting* , December (2001)]

Tubesing, EdD, Nancy Loving, and Donald A. Tubesing, PhD, *Kicking Your Holiday Stress Habits* (Duluth: Pfeifer-Hamilton Publishers, 1996).

Tucker, Kristin M., and Rebecca Lowe Warren, *Celebrate the Wonder, A Family Christmas Treasury* (New York: Ballantine/Epiphany Book, 1988).

Twigg, Nancy, *Celebrate Simply* (Knoxville: Counting the Cost Publications, 2003).

Varnum, Keith, "Survival Guide for the Holidays," www.theallineed.com.

"What is your best holiday travel tip?" *Real Simple Magazine,* December (2004).

Yates, Cynthia, *The Complete Guide to Creative Gift-Giving* (Ann Arbor: Servant Publications, 1997).

The Spirit of Simple Living™

by Sharon Hanby-Robie

The Simple Home

A Simple Christmas

The Spirit of Simple Living series offers uplifting titles that will help readers create a style of living that combines beauty and functionality with faith and spirituality. Join author Sharon Hanby-Robie as she shares inspiring narrative, real-life examples, and expert tips on how to live in the true spirit of simplicity.